ASHES 2023

ASHES 2023

A CRICKET CLASSIC

Gideon Haigh

SCRIBE
Melbourne • London

Scribe Publications
18–20 Edward St, Brunswick, Victoria 3056, Australia
2 John St, Clerkenwell, London, WC1N 2ES, United Kingdom
3754 Pleasant Ave, Suite 100, Minneapolis, Minnesota 55409, USA

Published by Scribe 2023

Printed and bound in the UK by CPI Group (UK) Ltd, Croydon
CR0 4YY

Scribe is committed to the sustainable use of natural resources and
the use of paper products made responsibly from those resources.

978 1 761380 90 7 (Australian edition)
978 1 915590 74 9 (UK edition)
978 1 761385 67 4 (ebook)

Catalogue records for this book are available from the
National Library of Australia and the British Library.

scribepublications.com.au
scribepublications.co.uk
scribepublications.com

CONTENTS

Foreword

BY PETER LALOR

A travelling Test cricket correspondent is tasked with summoning history's first draft of the day's events, filed at stumps, as most of the pieces in this collection are, and almost always without the benefit of hindsight or much reflection.

Gideon's first draft is inevitably the definitive take on the event. No more need be said; nothing need be added or amended. Get the book binder and assign a Dewey Decimal Classification to it.

I sometimes look across at him, always sitting beside me, and wonder what he is building in there as he variously strokes chin and keyboard. Bit by bit, he builds up a piece as the day progresses, vigilantly protective of the words on his screen. I have come to surmise that his is something of the Dadaist approach. Observations, sentences, paragraphs are crafted until the right note is struck, the right reference summoned, before being cut up and collated into that punk perfection — think *Hex Enduction Hour* — which is so distinctly and gloriously Gideon.

At least, I think that's what he does. I wouldn't dare ask, and I know he wouldn't consider telling me. Best, as the nuns told the girls at school, to retain a bit of mystery.

We chat about the day's events as they unfold (but mostly we digress); we dissect them later on the podcast (and again we digress); and while he does eventually relent and send me his story at the close of play, I do not read it until the next morning. What better way to start the day than with his account of the previous one, bound and ready for history's bookshelf? What worse way to end the day than to see how it should have been surmised?

I shouldn't give away too many press-box secrets, but there have been times, and there was at least one during the Ashes, when the rest of us hacks dust off a previous piece of Gideon's that is a particularly and humorously brutal assessment of a cricket incident. No matter how many times we have read it, it leaves us howling with laughter and simultaneously cringing for the victims—sorry, subjects. Those poor, sad bastards. Still, if you are going to be sliced to death, at the very least you'd want to be dissected by a master swordsman and not some hack with a machete.

Didn't you kill my brother, the family might ask, before pausing to note what a very nice job you did of it. (Apologies to Alexei Sayle.)

Within hours of his assessment of the Long Room fracas being published, I had a half-a-dozen people relate to me how much they enjoyed his description of the 'puce-faced, dim-bulb snobs', and by the end of the series I'd started to wonder whether the words would be included in Australia's Declaration of the Republic.

I could count on one hand the writers alive today who share Gideon's ability to coin, craft, and turn a phrase. It does him a disservice, however, not to acknowledge how this talent is used to bring the game and its characters to life, and to give the same a previously unconsidered context. His are not pretty words without purpose.

Usman Khawaja's batting, we are told here, is 'so self-sufficient he would not have been disturbed had his partner burst into flames'. 'Khawaja … tackles batting as he tackles life, at a steady pace.' His is a 'doctrine of minimalism'. 'With a touch here, a chip there, and orthodoxy everywhere, he controlled the innings' tempo like a silky midfielder. In defence, he quickly drops a hand from the bat as though to cushion the blow. Even his cross-bat shots have a sense of violence contained. He moves so minimally pigeons could roost on him', he writes of Khawaja's century at Edgbaston.

We all know the batsman and his craft better for Gideon having focused and framed him such, just as I could never not see Nathan Lyon as a Giacometti-type figure after he was described so by my eloquent friend.

Gideon's pop-culture references range in this collection from LS Lowry to Logan Roy. His account of Ben Stokes' field placings at Lord's is sublime: 'Nowhere in the MCC coaching manual or *The Jubilee Book of Cricket* will you encounter a fielding diagram of no slips, one gully, extra cover, fine third man, and a loose daisy chain of four on the on side reinforced by forward square leg on the fence. It looked more like what you might find on Google Maps if you typed in "pharmacies near me".'

English punk band The Adverts had a song called 'Gary Gilmore's Eyes' written from the view of a transplant patient who wakes up to find they are the recipient of the executed killer's peepers. 'I'm looking through Gary Gilmore's eyes,' the agonised protagonist sings, and while that may be a mixed bag, we are singularly blessed to see the game through Gideon Haigh's eyes.

I have said in the past that working with him is like batting with Bradman, but it does not do justice to the 360-degree delight that accompanies spending almost every waking minute of the day with such a good friend and such a gifted observer of the game. We have found ourselves in TS Eliot's rats' alley in the middle of a Manchester night, staring up at mosaics of Gideon's muse, Mark E Smith; we have visited everything from museums to sewers, and, combining those interests, a toilet museum (in Delhi); travelled second class on Indian trains; and beamed like fools as we boarded a mini railway carriage and spent hour after hour astride Shank's pony, lost here, or wandering there, always setting out early to distant grounds and usually wandering in late from darkened pubs or restaurants, where we would work ourselves up to states of irrational indignation before inevitably dissolving into fits of snorting laughter.

Rarely, in these hours, do we talk of the game; always, when we do, the subject shifts reflexively to some song we've heard, a show we've seen, a painting we like, or something that the other must not live another second without being informed of. As exhaustion sets in, as it surely does when you spend 50-odd days on the road, we find ourselves guffawing in various gutters and gullies, unable to take our self-pity seriously, but all the better for having someone to share it with.

Everyone should have a friend like Gideon, but at least we all have Gideon to elevate and illuminate what we all experienced collectively. The shared experience is always enhanced once he has crafted and recalibrated it for us, as he does in this collection.

Introduction

High hopes were held for the 2023 Ashes. They were exceeded. The series attained the status of a classic, holding interest on both sides of the world until the final delivery. The margins of victory: two wickets and 43 runs in Australia's favour, then three wickets and 49 runs in England's, testify to the tautness of the competition; the only truly one-sided match, ironically, was drawn. But even this fails to convey the drama arising from the contrast in approaches: from the outset, Pat Cummins' Australians were made to feel like they were truly *defending* the Ashes, were being attacked from all sides. Their cautious, organised, and disciplined cricket, the cricket that had won them the World Test Championship, faced a kind of ideological challenge from an English team imbued with the spirit of their earthy, up-and-at-'em captain Ben Stokes.

One felt the wheel turning: a Sixth Test, as favoured in England between 1981 and 1997, would have been a mouth-watering prospect. But, then, much had already been asked of the players, the series having been compressed into a month and a half by the exigencies of commerce. Two-all, only the third such scoreline since 1882, actually felt a satisfactory conclusion, gratifying the partisans of neither side — and these were much in evidence, most clearly during and after the Lord's Test.

Alex Carey's stumping of his opposite number Jonny Bairstow as England chased 371 on the final day will be debated till the crack of doom. There is, on its face, very little to dispute. Bairstow was clearly, and fairly, dismissed, wandering dozily out of his crease; such is elite sport's zero tolerance of inattention, whether it's a golfer failing to sign a scorecard or a runner making a false start. But it raked over the Ashes of ill-feeling, where Australia is regularly held to be too quick to take advantage and England too quick to take offence. It was almost as though fans of both countries had been waiting for a chance to call one another names: that they can do so without compunction is one of the freedoms of long association. But Marylebone Cricket Club will take a long time to live down the whiny petulance its members displayed that day, while the cloying banter of the respective prime ministers sapped one's will to live.

Ashes 2023 brings together real-time impressions, composed for *The Times* and *The Australian*, of what was my seventh visit to the Northern Hemisphere to report England hosting Australia. These are prefaced by overarching match reports written in arrears of each Test. I arrived at this formula for a book about the mighty Ashes of 2005: I prefer it to the magisterial hindsight of the tour books of yesteryear, partial to these as I remain. Test cricket is at its most enjoyable when it confounds your expectations, and 2023, like 2005, did so daily. Test cricket is further enriched when you're not only writing but podcasting, which I did for *Cricket Et Cetera* with my friend and colleague Peter Lalor. Pete and I have worked side by side for twelve years without a cross word, while also involved in a non-stop conversation about … well, stuff. Having never really intended to write cricket for a living, I've only really stuck it out this long because of him. Thanks, comrade. It's been real.

The World Test Championship Final

7 JUNE

Two cheers for the WTC

Cricket scheduling keeps finding ways to make itself a darker art. A final is, by definition, usually the last game one plays. But next week Australia will start its northern summer with a final, the World Test Championship, ahead of its most prestigious and storied series, the Ashes.

Yes, Australia, the number-one ranked Test nation, will play a single match against India, ranked number two, in what most fans will view as a warm-up to five matches against England, ranked number four. That this WTC final will be the first Test in 143 years The Oval has hosted in June is really one of the less weird things about it.

All this is occurring in arrears of the world's richest cricket event, the Indian Premier League, which is so old-fashioned that they still play the final at the end. The Tests are being squeezed up in order that the England Cricket Board devote August to its tenth-rate IPL knock-off, The Hundred. So here we are.

The prospect of Australia v India at The Oval should by rights be pleasing. No, let's be fair. It is pleasing, quite: here are two well-matched teams, consistently the best of the last two years and full of quality players, who can play five bowlers and still bat deep.

Their recent meeting in the Border-Gavaskar Trophy was undermined by shit-tip pitches, but The Oval seems to offer probably the fairest surface possible, with a hint that runs on the board will matter. In the venue's last ten Tests, the team batting first on winning the toss has won four times, drawn once, and lost once; the team fielding first on winning the toss has won twice and lost twice.

England took the latter course last year and bundled South Africa out for 118, but the Proteas' top order these days is like an Ikea kit without the instruction booklet. The northern summer has so far been dry, the skies look pretty clear for the next fortnight, and the average first innings score in the County Championship at The Oval has been around 300.

Australia may have the slightest edge. Pat Cummins' team will be the fresher, himself included. Steve Smith and Marnus Labuschagne have acclimatised in county cricket. The bowlers are well rested. The squad is at full strength, that ugly blow to Cameron Green's arm in his last IPL engagement having proven less serious than one first feared, while Scott Boland is the ideal proxy should Josh Hazlewood not come up.

India have both enormous experience, with Cheteshwar Pujara grinding runs out for Sussex lately, and ample flair, with Shubman Gill probably the world's hottest batting property at the moment. But they have lost four and drawn one of their last ten Tests abroad, even as their strength at home has grown—the two may not be unrelated. They still lack Jasprit Bumrah, Shreyas Iyer, and Rishabh Pant—perhaps indefinitely in the case of the last.

Which is why, I suspect, they will be sorely tempted to go into the final not with Pant's replacement during the Border-Gavaskar Trophy, KS Bharat, but Rohit Sharma's Mumbai Indians' exuberant opening partner, Ishan Kishan.

In India, Bharat rather failed to meet the standards of an elite gloveman; uncapped Ishan probably won't ever, but the brio of his left-handed batting is the nearest his country have to a like-for-like Pant substitute. Ishan's fourteen one-day internationals include a 131-ball 210 against Bangladesh six months ago, and his freedom at number seven would be enhanced by the presences of the Ravis, Jadeja, and Ashwin, at numbers six and eight. He's twenty-four, ripe and dauntless.

But again, to step back a little, what's discouraging about the World Test Championship final is that the occasion must be enjoyed, in the words of Viktor Frankl, in spite of everything. There is virtually no lead-in for expectation to build; there is no pause afterwards to savour its events or significance; four days separate it from the Edgbaston Test.

You must squint in such a way as to overlook that the World Test Championship itself is bonkers. One team has played as many as twenty-two Tests (England); others, as few as twelve (Bangladesh and Sri Lanka); and three other Test nations (Afghanistan, Zimbabwe, and Ireland) do not even compete, having been allotted a total of half-a-dozen Tests in the last two years. While Tests are traditionally played in series hosted by one nation or the other (viz the Ashes), the final is a one-off in a neutral venue, far from the fans of the participating countries, muting the overall effect, reducing a global showpiece to a boutique property.

Finally, the WTC final is another expression of cricket's devil's bargain. It depends for its commercial viability on India playing in the final, bringing some of its vast television audiences—even as the politically squalid Board of Control for Cricket in India connives to suck the marrow out of the rest of the international game.

So let's be absolutely frank as well as fair: as terrific as the cricketers will be on show from next Wednesday, as exciting as the potential of their rivalry, the WTC final is cricket's lip service to a format with a clouded future. Which is a thousand pities.

Cricket will pause momentarily, then revert to the far more pressing business of making money. After the Headingley Test, in fact, it will be time to tune in to the likes of the San Francisco Unicorns (captain Aaron Finch) and the Washington Freedom (captain Moises Henriques) in the US's Major League Cricket. I haven't checked, but imagine they will also have the final at the end.

Gimme Head

Pretty soon you will look up the word 'counterpunch' in the dictionary and find a photo of Travis Head. Since the start of the last Ashes, he has become Australia's beacon of bouncebackability, as hard to bowl to as David Warner in his pomp and nearly as reliable.

His 163 from 174 balls in the World Test Championship final, the first century in that fixture, has now taken this capability to the world, where previously it had been largely for home consumption—as reflected in a Test average in Australia of 58 and abroad of 27 going into the match. By the end of the Ashes, the gap should have narrowed further.

So what goes into a game like Head's, which Ben Stokes confided a week or so ago made him as challenging a rival as anyone in Australia's top six? 'He was so hard to bowl to in Australia when we were there last time [2021–22] because he just threw counterpunches,' said England's captain—no stranger to using opponents as speed bags.

'Counterpunching'—essentially the choice to attack when

the orthodox response to a scoreline might be to defend or consolidate—may be counterintuitive, but it is not illogical. Attacking field settings and bowling to wicket-seeking lengths are also favourable to enterprising batsmanship. So a bit of nerve can go a long way.

Head himself has also always been a batter harder to subdue than to get out. His maiden T20 hundred took 53 balls; he has made two List A double centuries. He relies on fast hands to make up for flat feet, but his attacking options are broad: he not only savages width, but owns anything bowled too straight; left-handedness and sharp running enhance his value further.

That makes for rapid impact, and the boundaries that Head peeled off through and over the leg side after coming in with Australia having lost three wickets in the first twenty-five overs of the innings on Wednesday seemed to turn the match in a trice.

After sixteen deliveries, Head was 27. Bowlers who had come into the match after two months of one-over and two-over spells in the Indian Premier League suddenly found themselves challenged to maintain consistency for anything longer.

The Oval's outfield is as frictionless as a polished mirror: Head would eventually hit twenty-four fours, one six, and only one three. But India had to keep attacking in order to justify their decisions to bowl first and to exclude Ravi Ashwin (who has dismissed Head thrice in six encounters—just saying).

Rohit Sharma's struggle to contain is reflected in the balls that Head took for each of his half-centuries: 60, 56, and 48.

Any prolonged innings by Head, it is also true, contains its share of miscues and misfires, and this was no exception. Between the powerful cuts, pulls, and punches, he scattered some wacky wafts and ham-fisted hooks.

Twice he was hit on the bonce; he nearly dragged on; he top-edged into space. When the ball was hip high, Head looked like he'd been administered a shock with an electric cattle prod. But his control percentage of 69 per cent proved less significant than his intent percentage of 100 per cent.

The South Australian reminds you of the phrase 'good bad books' that Orwell popularised for 'the kind of book that has no literary pretensions but which remains readable when more serious productions have perished'. For Head is a master of good bad batting. He lays no claim to easeful style or technical precision, yet has found a way to accumulate more than 10,000 first-class runs.

It is not only the moustache that lends Head a 1970s retro chic; the unself-conscious roughness of his technique has defied the homogenising influences of coached conformism and video self-scrutiny. Like Doug Walters, he can contribute useful overs also.

Stokes and Baz McCullum now have more counter-counterpunching to contemplate. With his reliance on boundaries, Head will likely find himself hemmed in with more defensive fields; with his propensity for closing off, he will cop a lot more along the body. His head-to-heads with Moeen Ali, now mooted as England's proxy for the injured Jack Leach, are unlikely to last long either way.

Early thought in England had been that the Labuschagne-Smith axis would prove the home team's most formidable obstacle in these Ashes. Australia's number five has now countered that, too.

SCOREBOARD

Final: The Oval, 7-11 June 2023
Australia: 469 & 270/8d

Toss: Australia
India: 296 & 234

Australia won by 209 runs

AUSTRALIA 1ST INNINGS

BATTING		R	B	M	4S	6S	SR
David Warner	c †Bharat b Thakur	43	60	108	8	0	71.66
Usman Khawaja	c †Bharat b Mohammed Siraj	0	10	15	0	0	0.00
Marnus Labuschagne	b Mohammed Shami	26	62	103	3	0	41.93
Steven Smith	b Thakur	121	268	333	19	0	45.14
Travis Head	c †Bharat b Mohammed Siraj	163	174	283	25	1	93.67
Cameron Green	c Shubman Gill b Mohammed Shami	6	7	15	1	0	85.71
Alex Carey †	lbw b Jadeja	48	69	98	7	1	69.56
Mitchell Starc	run out (sub [AR Patel])	5	20	24	0	0	25.00
Pat Cummins (c)	c Rahane b Mohammed Siraj	9	34	82	0	0	26.47
Nathan Lyon	b Mohammed Siraj	9	25	18	1	0	36.00
Scott Boland	not out	1	7	8	0	0	14.28
Extras	(b 13, lb 10, nb 7, w 8)	38					
TOTAL	121.3 Ov (RR: 3.86)	469					

Fall of wickets: 1-2 (Usman Khawaja, 3.4 ov), 2-71 (David Warner, 21.4 ov), 3-76 (Marnus Labuschagne, 24.1 ov), 4-361 (Travis Head, 91.1 ov), 5-376 (Cameron Green, 94.2 ov), 6-387 (Steven Smith, 98.1 ov), 7-402 (Mitchell Starc, 103.5 ov), 8-453 (Alex Carey, 114.4 ov), 9-468 (Nathan Lyon, 119.5 ov), 10-469 (Pat Cummins, 121.3 ov)

BOWLING	O	M	R	W	ECON	WD	NB
Mohammed Shami	29	4	122	2	4.20	1	2
Mohammed Siraj	28.3	4	108	4	3.78	3	1
Umesh Yadav	23	5	77	0	3.34	0	0
Shardul Thakur	23	4	83	2	3.60	0	4
Ravindra Jadeja	18	2	56	1	3.11	0	0

INDIA 1ST INNINGS

BATTING		R	B	M	4S	6S	SR
Rohit Sharma (c)	lbw b Cummins	15	26	29	2	0	57.69
Shubman Gill	b Boland	13	15	33	2	0	86.66
Cheteshwar Pujara	b Green	14	25	35	2	0	56.00
Virat Kohli	c Smith b Starc	14	31	56	2	0	45.16
Ajinkya Rahane	c Green b Cummins	89	129	254	11	1	68.99
Ravindra Jadeja	c Smith b Lyon	48	51	84	7	1	94.11
Srikar Bharat †	b Boland	5	15	21	0	0	33.33
Shardul Thakur	c †Carey b Green	51	109	156	6	0	46.78
Umesh Yadav	b Cummins	5	11	16	1	0	45.45
Mohammed Shami	c †Carey b Starc	13	11	23	2	0	118.18
Mohammed Siraj	not out	0	3	7	0	0	0.00
Extras	(b 10, lb 10, nb 8, w 1)	29					
TOTAL	69.4 Ov (RR: 4.24)	296					

Fall of wickets: 1-30 (Rohit Sharma, 5.6 ov), 2-30 (Shubman Gill, 6.4 ov), 3-50 (Cheteshwar Pujara, 13.5 ov), 4-71 (Virat Kohli, 18.2 ov), 5-142 (Ravindra Jadeja, 34.3 ov), 6-152 (Srikar Bharat, 38.2 ov), 7-261 (Ajinkya Rahane, 61.6 ov), 8-271 (Umesh Yadav, 65.5 ov), 9-294 (Shardul Thakur, 68.3 ov), 10-296 (Mohammed Shami, 69.4 ov)

BOWLING	O	M	R	W	ECON	WD	NB
Mitchell Starc	13.4	0	71	2	5.19	0	0
Pat Cummins	20	2	83	3	4.15	0	6
Scott Boland	20	6	59	2	2.95	0	0
Cameron Green	12	1	44	2	3.66	1	2
Nathan Lyon	4	0	19	1	4.75	0	0

AUSTRALIA 2ND INNINGS

BATTING		R	B	M	4S	6S	SR
Usman Khawaja	c †Bharat b Yadav	13	39	70	2	0	33.33
David Warner	c †Bharat b Mohammed Siraj	1	8	16	0	0	12.50
Marnus Labuschagne	c Pujara b Yadav	41	126	199	4	0	32.53
Steven Smith	c Thakur b Jadeja	34	47	68	3	0	72.34
Travis Head	c & b Jadeja	18	27	29	0	2	66.66
Cameron Green	b Jadeja	25	95	114	4	0	26.31
Alex Carey †	not out	66	105	162	8	0	62.85
Mitchell Starc	c Kohli b Mohammed Shami	41	57	80	7	0	71.92
Pat Cummins (c)	c sub (AR Patel) b Mohammed Shami	5	5	7	1	0	100.00
Extras	(b 9, lb 9, nb 2, w 6)	26					
TOTAL	84.3 Ov (RR: 3.19)	270/8d					

Did not bat: Nathan Lyon, Scott Boland

Fall of wickets: 1-2 (David Warner, 3.3 ov), 2-24 (Usman Khawaja, 14.1 ov), 3-86 (Steven Smith, 30.1 ov), 4-111 (Travis Head, 36.3 ov), 5-124 (Marnus Labuschagne, 46.4 ov), 6-167 (Cameron Green, 62.6 ov), 7-260 (Mitchell Starc, 82.6 ov), 8-270 (Pat Cummins, 84.3 ov)

BOWLING	O	M	R	W	ECON	WD	NB
Mohammed Shami	16.3	6	39	2	2.36	1	1
Mohammed Siraj	20	2	80	1	4.00	1	1
Shardul Thakur	8	1	21	0	2.62	0	0
Umesh Yadav	17	1	54	2	3.17	0	0
Ravindra Jadeja	23	4	58	3	2.52	0	0

INDIA 2ND INNINGS (T: 444 RUNS)

BATTING		R	B	M	4S	6S	SR
Rohit Sharma (c)	lbw b Lyon	43	60	103	7	1	71.66
Shubman Gill	c Green b Boland	18	19	40	2	0	94.73
Cheteshwar Pujara	c †Carey b Cummins	27	47	68	5	0	57.44
Virat Kohli	c Smith b Boland	49	78	115	7	0	62.82
Ajinkya Rahane	c †Carey b Starc	46	108	161	7	0	42.59
Ravindra Jadeja	c †Carey b Boland	0	2	1	0	0	0.00
Srikar Bharat †	c & b Lyon	23	41	77	2	0	56.09
Shardul Thakur	lbw b Lyon	0	5	6	0	0	0.00
Umesh Yadav	c †Carey b Starc	1	12	12	0	0	8.33
Mohammed Shami	not out	13	8	17	3	0	162.50
Mohammed Siraj	c Boland b Lyon	1	6	9	0	0	16.66
Extras	(lb 2, nb 5, w 6)	13					
TOTAL	63.3 Ov (RR: 3.68)	234					

Fall of wickets: 1-41 (Shubman Gill, 7.1 ov), 2-92 (Rohit Sharma, 19.5 ov), 3-93 (Cheteshwar Pujara, 20.4 ov), 4-179 (Virat Kohli, 46.3 ov), 5-179 (Ravindra Jadeja, 46.5 ov), 6-212 (Ajinkya Rahane, 56.2 ov), 7-213 (Shardul Thakur, 57.4 ov), 8-220 (Umesh Yadav, 60.2 ov), 9-224 (Srikar Bharat, 61.5 ov), 10-234(Mohammed Siraj, 63.3 ov)

BOWLING	O	M	R	W	ECON	WD	NB
Pat Cummins	13	1	55	1	4.23	1	4
Scott Boland	16	2	46	3	2.87	0	0
Mitchell Starc	14	1	77	2	5.50	0	1
Cameron Green	5	0	13	0	2.60	1	0
Nathan Lyon	15.3	2	41	4	2.64	0	0

Australia, temporarily, rules the world

Australia have not merely won the World Test Championship. They have dominated it. Only rain prevented their winning every home Test in its two-year cycle; they split their away Tests, which is about as well as anyone does these days; they monstered their nearest rival, India, in the neutral final.

Pat Cummins' team averaged 10 more with bat than ball. Usman Khawaja, Marnus Labuschagne, Steve Smith, and Travis Head were among the top six scorers. Nathan Lyon, Pat Cummins, and Mitchell Starc were in the top six wicket takers. Perhaps the effect is diffuse for being spread over two years, and intermingled with white ball distractions, but it's also inarguable.

The Australians were probably not quite at their best at The Oval. Catches went down; wickets fell to no balls; extras were conceded. But there is a long peak for them to sustain in this northern summer, and in the perpetual trade-off of preparation against future endurance, the Australians probably got the balance as right as you can.

India, not so much. In fact, they were far, far poorer than they should have been. Australia learned in 2019 that you abdicate first innings at The Oval at your peril; India got distracted by a few clouds. The exclusion of Ravi Ashwin was a howler, Rohit Sharma's admonition to play with 'freedom' a cop-out, the bowling plans pretty much non-existent, and there was altogether too much 'all right on the night' thinking.

Still, if you elect to play your home Tests on a succession of rank turners, be prepared to suffer the consequence on surfaces where the balance between bat and ball is more even. India looked like a team that would like to have won the World Test Championship final if they could get it on their terms, or Jay Shah could get it for them, rather than one prepared to make genuine sacrifices to do so.

Which Australia was. They wanted it, and badly. Inattention to over rates had cost them their chance to play in the first final; this cycle, they left nothing to chance. They fought back, too. Pantsed at Nagpur and Delhi earlier this year, shuffled to Indore, deprived of Cummins by circumstances, and of David Warner, Josh Hazlewood, and Cameron Green by injury, relying on two junior spinners and an ersatz opening combination, they made sure of their final berth by winning the Third Test of the Border-Gavaskar Trophy—in hindsight, as meritorious a win as any in the cycle by anyone.

Why did they want it? Precisely because they value the format. Lots of fans out there purport to 'love' Test cricket. The Australian team make this love real. Stop and listen to them some time. When they talk about their Test performances, it is almost always in terms of the excitement at its particular demands, its paramount significance in determining a cricketer's prowess.

'No doubt Test matches for us are our favourite format,' said Cummins in the aftermath of victory at The Oval. 'It's the biggest challenge I think in every way. This competition, pitting up against everyone in the world, it has got to be right up there.'

In every media interaction, this is a team that speaks with one voice. Steve Smith calls Test cricket 'a great format of the game, and it's something that I love playing'; Nathan Lyon argues that 'to get your baggy green and play Test cricket for a long time, that's the absolute ultimate.'

Marnus Labuschagne, typically, is never slow to accentuate the positive. 'In the last three, four years it [Test cricket] has been unbelievable,' he said a few weeks ago. 'It's been so entertaining. The 2019 Ashes was an unbelievable series. Australia v India in Australia, *really* good series. We just had a pretty good series in India on some diabolical turning wickets, and then you go New Zealand v England, Pakistan v England. I mean, the game's coming alive.'

Even David Warner in setting himself to retire in a Test match has accorded the format a priority, while there was some pressure on Cameron Green when he took the Indian Premier League shilling not to do so at the expense of his long-term Test prospects.

At the same time, the players are under no illusions. When a *Guardian* interviewer recently estimated that Mitchell Starc had forsaken $15 million by resisting the siren song of franchise cricket, he responded: 'The traditionalist in me still hopes there is a generation of boys and girls who want to represent their country in Test cricket. But the easy money is in franchise cricket, it's the fast track to notoriety.'

These perspectives are encouraging, if you value Test cricket, and also something for which the players deserve more credit from the game's more tedious jeremiahs, with their unexamined assumptions that cricket these days, like everything else, is just a load of woke rubbish.

'Test cricket is still the pinnacle,' said Lyon a few weeks ago. 'It is the only format where you cannot hide ... I'm definitely not concerned about the future of Test cricket, but it's on players, not just administrators, to ensure it has a future.' Don't know about you, but he sounds pretty sincere to me.

Which is another reason why this summer's Ashes loom so large, because perhaps the only other team in world cricket who talk up Test cricket as much as Australia is ... England.

'Test cricket is something that needs to be looked after,' said Ben Stokes earlier this year. 'We don't want Test cricket to fall off the face of the planet. It needs to stay around, and we'll do everything we possibly can as a team to keep it alive.'

It is no small thing that Stokes, who has starred in the finals of a 50-over and a 20-over World Cup, argues that there remains 'no greater privilege than to represent your country in a Test match'. Bazball is, among other things, a reminder to remain unburdened by that privilege; to enjoy it. That bodes well for us, because if they're enjoying it, we are bound to.

The Ashes
in Prospect

14 JUNE

The teams line up

After the toss but before play at Edgbaston on 16 June, the teams will appear in front of the pavilion. It's an opportunity to see who likes singing along with the national anthem; also to study the form, as it were, in the mounting yard. Who is there? How do they look? How do they appear relative to each other?

The names of the England team we know, it being an artefact of Bazball confidence that they are always named a day or two out: it's been confirmed that the breakdown of Jack Leach has led to the shout-out for the retired Moeen Ali; Stuart Broad's five for 51 in the first innings against Ireland at Lord's, we now learn, has given him the edge over other candidates for the last seamer's position. Of Australia, we know basically the shape: it is likely, but not certain, that Scott Boland will retain his place from the World Test Championship final; there is some hint that Josh Hazlewood will return in place of Mitchell Starc after the latter's scrappy outing in the same game. So the evidence for judgement is reasonable.

Australia, then, will have the experience edge. They will be more or less the same team that finished the 2021–22 Ashes, and in the same roles and places — that stability a reflection of success in the interim. All the batters have hundreds in their last five Tests; all the bowlers, save Boland, have five-fers in the last six months. Hazlewood is the sole player with a chequered fitness record, his physique having perhaps been stressed by his pursuit of T20 success; Cameron Green is recovered from the broken finger that kept him on the outer for much of the Border-Gavaskar Trophy.

They're an impressive unit, as well they might be, considering their recent WTC laurels, so that one must go looking for concerns. David Warner is on his fourth Ashes tour still in search of a hundred; Marnus Labuschagne has played sixteen away Tests and made only one; Steve Smith may not be quite the player he was four years ago, when he made 774 runs in the Ashes. Although who is?

Anyway, they're a known quantity—as known, perhaps, as England is unknown. Four of the home team's top five—Zak Crawley, Ben Duckett, Ollie Pope, and Harry Brook—have played six Ashes Tests between them. Moeen Ali has not played a Test in almost two years, and another first-class match in almost four; Jonny Bairstow (recovering from a broken leg) missed England's winter tours; Ben Stokes (suffering a damaged knee) was confined to two matches in the Indian Premier League; James Anderson and Ollie Robinson both picked up injuries in the early rounds of the County Championship; and Mark Wood is apparently not yet over a chronic elbow problem.

Of these, the role of wicketkeeper seems the most worrying proposition. Ben Foakes had been keeping and batting to a high standard, while the Ireland Test and two Division Two county matches hardly seem enough for Bairstow to prepare for the rigours of wearing the gloves for potentially a day and more—which Test match cricket involves. Bairstow was a good but never great keeper, and has not performed the task in a Test for nearly five years. What could possibly go wrong?

What England do have is an ethos. Bazball was, of course, so designated by a journalist for their newly arrived coach, Baz McCullum, after hints of a fresh approach to Test cricket by Stokes' team in the early days of their combination a year ago. But it might have been retrospectively dubbed Bayball: after all, it was Trevor Bayliss who, between 2015 and 2019, encouraged Eoin Morgan's English white-ball side to let go the reins on their natural flair, spurring them to World Cup success.

McCullum's contribution, I suspect, was to see the potential pent up in England's Test cricket, for which he had a particular eye, having only ever coached white-ball teams. And he was free to license a similar approach in red-ball cricket because every other method had failed — failure mandates change, just as success sometimes stifles it.

Bazball will never have a sterner examination than this summer, against the most disciplined, cohesive, and thriftiest team around. Five Tests will mitigate its shock value, allow for the development of disruptive strategies, and with the best will in the world take some toll on its practitioners: how you play on a fresh field is different from how you play with two or three failures behind you. Injuries will crop up; replacements will need to be assimilated.

But some evidence is in already. England play better with Bazball than without: they have won eleven of thirteen Tests, versus one of seventeen before then. And you needn't look at anyone in either team to know that against Australia any approach would represent an improvement on 2021–22.

15 JUNE

Australia v Bazball

'You going to have a crack today?' Thus Australia's Brad Haddin as Brendon McCullum took guard in the 2015 World Cup final at the MCG. New Zealand's captain had laid waste to one attack after another in that tournament; his fortunes looked likely to shape the climactic match.

McCullum grunted assent, Mitchell Starc stormed in, and the latter yorked the former with his third ball. New Zealand recoiled; Australia surged; and the match almost condensed to that first contest.

So while Starc, Steve Smith, David Warner, and Josh Hazlewood may be yet to experience the full withering blast of Bazball, they can claim to have seen off a brush with an earlier version, when the harder they swung, the bigger they fell.

Eight years on, the approach of throwing a gauntlet down against Australia will again be on trial, with McCullum now a plotter — a fine cricketer and shrewd thinker who, nonetheless, was only once in sixteen Tests against Australia on the winning side.

England's commitment is bound to outlast New Zealand's that fateful day. This, arguably, is the point to it: the attack comes in waves rather than spasms; it does not hold back; it does not wait its turn. But it has been intriguing to watch their Ashes rival assimilate this new dash of the old enemy over the last year, in which Ben Stokes' Englishmen have carried all before them on the Test field. For Australia remains the last refuge of the Bazball sceptic.

In the early days of England's risorgimento, if you recall, McCullum himself scorned mention of Bazball, averse to the notion he had somehow personally mandated it. Gradually he has relaxed his objection—partly because there's no catching a media hare once it has started running, and partly because it has value as an expression of collective purpose, a combination of brand and mission statement.

Its attractiveness is as obvious as Danny Blanchflower's immortal lines, which apply to cricket as well as football: 'The game is about glory, it is about doing things in style and with a flourish, about going out and beating the lot, not waiting for them to die of boredom.' Who would not wish to fall in with such an ethos? Especially when it is cast in the image of a cricketer, Stokes, so compelling and so beloved.

In their selection for the First Test, moreover, they have doubled down: out with the superior stumper Ben Foakes in favour of the superior striker Jonny Bairstow; with the injury to full-time spinner and doughty blocker Jack Leach, there is a recall for the languid strokeplay and speculative off-breaks of Moeen Ali.

But Bazball's appeal against Australia is doubly obvious. For Australia's factory setting is a kind of earthy audacity, which Fred Spofforth and Billy Murdoch would surely have christened OzBall had the Victorian age understood the power of a hashtag. Sir Leonard Hutton later summed Australian teams up so: 'They have the utmost ability for producing that little extra, or instilling into the opposition an inferiority complex that can have and has had a crushing effect. Australians have no inhibitions.' What sport to turn the tables on England's eternal tormenter with cricket similarly uninhibited.

Not that it's quite the same. Australian aggression has tended to be anterior to results. That combination of steamroller and parade float driven by Mark Taylor and Steve Waugh in the nineties and noughties gradually expanded their attacking ambitions from a base of success. England has come to a new way of thinking only after experiencing failure every other way.

Thus a nagging Australian sense that England has fallen for a kind of crypto-cricket—new and exciting, but meretricious and ultimately unsound. When your top three are Warner, Usman Khawaja, and Marnus Labuschagne, it is tempting to regard Ben Duckett, Zak Crawley, and Ollie Pope as Logan Roy did his offspring—'not serious people'.

The Australians have deflected Bazball questions so far on tour, politely but guardedly. 'So, you know, they've obviously done well against other attacks,' said Smith a couple of weeks ago. 'But they haven't come up against us yet.' Likewise Starc: 'If they are five for 50, are they still coming out and swinging? Dunno.'

Last week, Waugh himself, progenitor of the 400-run Test day, pitched in: 'That is the big question mark over so-called Bazball. What is Plan B? Have they got a Plan B? If they haven't then they are going to be found out.' I loved that grudging 'so-called', and the recommendation of a Plan B from a skipper who seldom needed to vary his rinse-and-repeat Plan A.

Australian teams coming to England have been overconfident before, notably in 2005 and 2015. There is enough common sense in this group not to succumb to the same vice: they are the first to point out Australia's failure to win an away Ashes outright since 2001, which provides them with their own sense of mission.

But England's recent mantle as Test cricket's pacesetter will be a challenge to Australian *amour propre*, and they will seize on the first evidence of it fraying at the edges. They will relish succeeding against it; they will certainly not wish to be seen as giving in to it. And they certainly won't need to ask whether England will be having a crack.

The First Test: Edgbaston

16–20 June 2023
Australia won by two wickets

Birmingham sixes

The World Test Championship final at The Oval had been an excellent Test match. Within a week of ending, it had been almost forgotten. Such was the pageant of skill, event, and fluctuation in the First Test at Edgbaston, England throwing everything at Australia, and Australia somehow catching it—sometimes in the tips of their fingers and between their legs, but catching it all the same. Despite looking in desperate straits at stages, Australia kept its first-innings deficit within bounds, prevented England from running riot in the third innings, and magicked a win late on the final day by means of a 55-run ninth-wicket stand in 72 balls by captain Pat Cummins and old lag Nathan Lyon. Lyon, whose tenacity with the ball had kept Australia in touch throughout, can hardly have led the Australian team song more proudly.

The game was preluded by the usual nonsense preliminaries, pyrotechnics as spectacular as the gas jets on a barbecue. The fireworks really began with the first ball: a fifth-stump loosener from Cummins driven on the up through cover by the towering Zak Crawley who, after the early loss of Ben Duckett, dominated the initial exchanges, in which England took their first 100 from 122 balls. This was more than usually important. Australia had excluded their fastest bowler, Mitchell Starc, in favour of their most reliable, Scott Boland, and started with defensive fields that grew ever more introverted: third slip lasted two overs, and Nathan Lyon bowled the tenth over with four men on the fence. But neither these nor even the fall of wickets did anything to quell the flow of forty fours and five sixes in 78 overs. As wave after wave followed, there was nowhere further to fall back to.

Almost eight years on from his last Ashes hundred, Joe Root was the dominant figure, his reverse ramps for six off Cummins and Boland a motif of freedom, his 31st Test century an afternoon delight. Harry Brook was unluckily bowled, the ball from Nathan Lyon bouncing over his body as he played no shot. But, with England five for 176, Jonny Bairstow provided the kind of spiky and spunky innings in which England had invested, helping Root put on 121 in 140 balls for the sixth wicket. Root had just taken two more sixes off Lyon down the ground when Stokes provided the Bazballsiest moment of all, calling his men in so as to fit in a four-over crack at Australia's openers. It bore no fruit, but meant that England enjoyed the advantage of starting their next day's bowling under mackerel skies, whereupon Stuart Broad, who had won the last place in England's pace attack when Mark Wood reported short of full fitness, removed David Warner and Marnus Labuschagne in consecutive balls. When Stokes trapped Steve Smith, Australia was a painstaking three for 67 in 27 overs.

Cometh the hour, cometh Usman: Khawaja, on his third Ashes tour, finally made his first real impact, with batting so self-sufficient he would not have been disturbed had his partners burst into flames. In fact, the South Australians Head and Alex Carey helped add 81 (113 balls) and 118 (192 balls) respectively, though England would have been a great deal better off had Broad not castled Khawaja (on 112) with a no ball and had the ungainly Bairstow not failed to stump Cameron Green (on 0) off

Moeen. Moeen's soft spinning finger was rubbed raw by the stress of 33 overs, Ollie Robinson's soft head was confirmed by the sour send-off he gave Khawaja on bowling him, and England's second innings was delayed into an abbreviated third day when both openers were removed by the new ball under overcast skies.

With Ollie Pope and then Harry Brook, Joe Root was progressing breezily on the fourth morning when England relieved the pressure again. Root chose the moment to be stumped off Lyon for the first time in his Test career, whereupon Brook hit fretfully to mid-wicket, and Bairstow played fatally back. After Stokes was trapped on the crease in an excellent spell by his opposite number, sixty-three useful runs came from the last three wickets, but England really needed an early breakthrough in Australia's second innings — which they did not get when Bairstow, again, let an outside edge from Khawaja pass between him and Root at first slip in the first over. Khawaja then led a sound start with David Warner, although Broad's vintage closing spell to remove Labuschagne and Smith left the hosts needing seven wickets on the last day and the visitors 174 runs.

Achieving the rare feat of batting on every day of a Test, Khawaja prolonged his long vigil into the last afternoon with a series of useful if not definitive partnerships. When Stokes went through his defence after he had batted for nearly 800 minutes in the match, England finally seemed to have taken the upper hand, and tightened their grip when Root held onto a hot caught-and-bowled from Carey with the new ball in the offing. Stokes gambled with an extra over from his part-timer with no outfield; Cummins gambled back, twice hitting over the top for six. Lyon took a chance, too, hooking at Broad with two men back, but Stokes failed to complete the catch, leaping with a single hand, and the new ball came sweetly from the cheerfully swung bats. Lyon's airy drives down the ground off Broad narrowed the gap, and Cummins' solid clumps from Robinson closed it, his guide to third man bisecting Crawley and Brook amid scenes of general celebration.

'Both teams spoke a lot about playing your own style', Cummins said afterwards. 'And that's the beauty of this series. Two contrasting styles, playing to our strengths, and that made for great entertainment.' Nor was Stokes for turning: 'A loss is a loss. We've said how we were going to operate. Losing hurts and winning is a great feeling. We're going to keep making moves if we feel the time is right and if we end up on the wrong side of results like this, there won't be much to complain about.' And there wasn't.

16 JUNE

Day 1

The maiden is one of cricket's uniquenesses, in that it involves the recording of nothing happening: six scoreless deliveries which need not even be of especial merit. But it contains a kind of cricket truth: that just as less can be more, nothing can be something. And the lack of nothing can be a problem.

Josh Hazlewood's ninth over at Edgbaston yesterday, the 37th of England's innings, was a maiden — to six full, straightish deliveries, Harry Brook offered five firm defensive bats and a leave. Much later, an over bowled by Nathan Lyon was blocked out by newly arrived Ollie Robinson.

And, errr, that's it. Australia's bowlers pride themselves on their thrift. More than a quarter of the Test overs of Hazlewood, Pat Cummins, and Scott Boland have been maidens; with Nathan Lyon, the proportion has been nearly a fifth. Australia's selectors make much ado of nothing, too. They excluded Mitchell Starc here out of worry at his occasional waywardness.

Their control did not increase proportionally, if not for want of trying. Despite Cummins setting fields so negative they were almost inert, England fairly clattered along, achieving a fluency they never threatened in the previous Ashes, when they were not only dismissed for fewer than 200 on six occasions, but limped everywhere at barely 3 an over.

The contrast could hardly have come more quickly. Zak Crawley, a columnar figure pervading off stump with all 196 of his centimetres, powered Cummins' first ball on the up to the extra cover boundary: a bugle blast to commence the boundary hunt.

Australia had come prepared, and Cummins did not so much revert to defence as embark from it. Within a few overs, more fielders were patrolling the perimeter than lurking in the cordon—an umbrella field of a different kind, complete with sou'wester and oilskin coat, as a precaution against a deluge of boundaries.

It flushed out the up-and-at-'em brigade, as ever, although one hardly recalls the same criticism of Michael Vaughan, whose sweepers in 2005 were similarly designed to limit the Australians' boundary flow. I know, I know: nobody should give up the 'attacking Aussie' cliché lightly. Take anything you like; just leave us our stereotypes. But, frankly, the skies were so clear and the surface so slow that slips were almost ornamental anyway: an early nick of Crawley's barely carried two-thirds of the way to Smith, who conspicuously came up a pace, coaxing Warner to come forward also.

After a few early boundaries, a pattern emerged, for England was quite prepared to exploit the vistas that Cummins' fields opened if they couldn't reach the fence as often as they have been used to. There were seventy-seven scoring shots before lunch for 124 runs: 1.6 runs per stroke. England were throwing punches, Australia limiting their impact, and in gaining three knockdowns earned points from the judges. Crawley's edge behind on the stroke of lunch gave each team a share of the round … errr, session.

There were first glimpses of Bazball bravura after lunch, with Harry Brook chafing to get down the pitch to the pace bowlers, and doing so to the slow: Boland and Lyon were launched inside-out over cover. England's prodigy was twenty-four off 20 balls when Boland threw one out so wide that Brook needed to telescope his arms to make contact—not so much rope-a-dope bowling as rope-a-steer. Head, however, misjudged the top edge, missed the catch, and soon after allowed an offside boundary he shouldn't have: the hosts were in danger of breaking free.

It's no coincidence that around the time Hazlewood bowled his precious maiden, Australia had its best twenty-minute interlude. Lyon removed a luckless Brook, and Hazlewood a heedless Stokes. Another wicket hereabouts and we might now be saluting Cummins' tactical acumen. It did not come. Joe Root, who has seemed a willing conscript to Bazball rather than an enthusiastic volunteer, reached a timely accommodation with it—it is only a slight exaggeration to say that he hits harder reverse than orthodox. Lyon placed first one then two fielders to counteract his backhanded sweeps; twice his riotous reverse ramps sailed for six over third man before he shovelled two further sixes down the ground.

Jonny Bairstow took up batting at number seven what he left off at number five, after ten innings in that slot with only one half-century. He left runs out there, as did Moeen and Broad, who, with five men on the rope, need not have tried to clear it, but no force on earth was capable of preventing Root's long-delayed fourth Ashes century. The declaration, equally, was in tune with Stokes' desire to be the summer's tempo-setter.

Australia enjoyed one salutary dose of nothing, with David Warner and Usman Khawaja seeing their team through the final four overs without loss. But if more pitches like these are in prospect this summer, nothing is going to come into its own. It reminds me a little of Percival Everett's new metaphysical caper comedy *Dr No*, in which a supervillain bent on wicked ends seeks to harness the power of nothing. He is abetted, then resisted, by a mathematician who is a nothing expert, and who is persuaded that the best counter is to have no plan. 'You're saying I should give them nothing?' he asks a confidante. 'As much of it as you can get,' comes the reply. After today, Pat Cummins may be feeling the same way.

Stumps: England 1st innings 393/8 (decl). Australia 1st innings 14/0 (David Warner 8*, Usman Khawaja 4*, 4 ov)

17 JUNE

Day 2

Usman Khawaja keeps finding new worlds to conquer. Some are well and truly familiar. Yesterday at Edgbaston was his fifteenth Test innings in England spread over a decade. He had averaged less than 20, with a solitary half-century. In some respects, his undefeated 126, a seventh hundred since returning to the colours, was less a surprise than the previous underperformance.

Khawaja has never at any stage in his career looked other than a player of quality. But his first eight years in international cricket were so uneven as to make his last eighteen months as Australia's most reliable batter an exercise in redress.

Coolly, composedly, he has gone back, ironing the kinks. Couldn't bat in Sri Lanka? Forget about that one. A sitting duck in India? Check that off. Gifted but lazy? A lazy cricketer does not bat more than ten hours in sapping heat as Khawaja did in Ahmedabad three months ago.

Yesterday, Australia owed him everything. With a touch here, a chip there, and orthodoxy everywhere, he controlled the innings' tempo like a silky midfielder. In defence, he quickly drops a hand from the bat as though to cushion the blow. Even his cross-bat shots have a sense of violence contained. He moves so minimally that pigeons could roost on him.

The only departure from this doctrine of minimalism yesterday was Khawaja's celebration of his milestone, where he tossed his bat in the air, danced a little hornpipe of glee, and failed only to pull his jumper over his head ... then, a moment later, was leaning on his bat, serenity restored.

This was a fine hundred, for it is hardly a click-and-collect surface: the batter must make the pace, the length ball can only be driven with caution, the short ball is inclined to trampoline and even reach the keeper on the second bounce; such is the square's dustiness, the crease lines are in constant danger of disappearance. Australia might have been slow by comparison with England, but 3.3 an over was satisfactory headway, especially after they played twenty-four balls before opening their scoring.

This was a deep breath after the previous day's panting, although there was quickly another gasp of action. David Warner, caught between the priority of survival and the desire to assert, dragged Broad on. Then Marnus Labuschagne, who has made the judicious leave his hallmark in the last four years, crowded his off stump as though trying to insert himself into a half-heard conversation. Although his bat ended up well ahead of his body and outside the line, this was a failure of composure rather than of technique per se—a lovely, tantalising outswinger from Broad also.

Nor does Bazball become Bazzzzzball in the field. As captain, Ben Stokes never leaves the game alone—he is perpetually shaping, gesturing, suggesting, and cajoling. On Friday, it was the quicksilver declaration, and the preference for Broad for the new ball. On Saturday, it was extracting England's first twenty-seven overs from seven bowlers, including cameos from the part-timers Harry Brook and Joe Root; James Anderson, England's most venerable bowler, delivered only six of the first forty-eight overs.

The most popular spell was the opportune burst from himself.

At first, Stokes rather coasted in, only gradually opening the throttle of his muscle-car physique, before trapping a perplexed Steve Smith in front. The most considered overs were the twenty-nine at the Birmingham End allocated to Moeen Ali, who had bowled only twenty-six overs in the entire Indian Premier League — a generous invitation, like an offer from Stokes to stay in his spare room. Just when you were wondering whether Moeen might have been overstaying his welcome, the off spinner coaxed a casual shot from Head, and should have had Green stumped second ball.

Stokes' fields, meanwhile, are not so much funky as jazzy: improvisatory, anticipatory, infinitely adjustable, but with an underlying logic. Saturday morning, it was the twin leg slips for Smith, the short cover for Khawaja; Saturday afternoon, it was silly point for Head, short mid-off and mid-on for Green. Then, of course, there are the fields he does not set, like the protective men in the deep for slow bowlers.

Having made the running, however, England were confounded by their own sloppiness — perhaps a corollary of Bazball, which in its grand sweeps and freedom from dreary consequences implicitly discourages a sweating of the small stuff. Bairstow had a poor day behind the stumps: he is as mobile as a sight screen. Broad and Stokes had an inattentive day on the front line: bowl as many as a dozen no balls, and chances are that you will cost yourself a wicket.

Had Bairstow accepted a regulation nick from Carey (26) and had Broad legitimately bowled Khawaja (112) in his first over with the second new ball, Australia would have been more than 120 runs adrift with a long tail to come.

With their sixth-wicket partnership at stumps having grown to 91 from 164 balls, Carey (46) surviving another chance at the wicket, the Australians could be satisfied at hanging on despite minimal contributions from their three best-credentialed batters: Smith, Warner and Labuschagne. From unpromising beginnings, good signs for the visitors. From the excellent, the better yet for one visitor in particular.

Stumps: Australia 1st innings 311/5 (Usman Khawaja 126*, Alex Carey 52*, 94 ov)

18 JUNE

Day 3

The two men had not previously met when, in June 1964, they rendezvoused at the Brown Bear in Whitechapel. But Tom Veivers and Jim Laker had something important in common: Veivers was Australia's best finger spinner of the time, Laker perhaps the greatest of all.

Their go-between had been Veivers' countryman and Laker's old rival Keith Miller. Veivers, a burly, rubicund Queenslander, had struggled with the English cold and the lacerating seams of English cricket balls. With the modest attack at his disposal, captain Bob Simpson had been depending on Veivers' capacities as a stock bowler: that capability was now in jeopardy.

When I interviewed Tom some decades later, he still had the scrap of paper on which Laker had furnished, one imagines with all the furtiveness of a spy imparting a nuclear secret, his hand-hardening formula for spinning success: 85 per cent pure alcohol, 10 per cent formalin, and 5 per cent surgical spirit.

It was quite a gesture in an Ashes series, especially given its subsequent efficacy. No Australian has bowled more first-class overs on a post-war Ashes tour than Tom, 754.5, including an Ashes record spell in Manchester of 95.1–36–153–3: enough to make a statto weep with joy. So there you are, Moeen: cricket may change in sixty years, but fingers haven't, so maybe the ancients have something to offer the moderns after all.

For the moment, one suspects, it is too late for Moeen's raw finger. His desperate remedies—a 'drying agent' applied on the field to relieve his injury—have cost him a quarter of his match fee, a demerit point, and a deal of his prospective effectiveness for the rest of this match.

Too many other factors are at play for Moeen's finger to be deemed the Edgbaston version of Cleopatra's nose—that coinage of Pascal's for the inconsequential detail with vital impact. ('Had Cleopatra's nose been shorter, the whole face of the world would have been changed.') But it is an unlucky charm: when Moeen began to loop up painful full tosses yesterday, one was reminded of his misfortunes at the top of his last Ashes series, when he arrived with a tender finger that quickly wore out.

Not every slow bowler ends up suffering similarly: Shane Warne's fingers remained soft and pliable his whole career, on account of his uncannily loose grip on the ball. But most spinners worth the name end up with finger joints embossed in corns and calluses from the friction involving in rotating the ball.

They either soldier on, like Warne's old mucka Tim May, who used to bowl on with bloody fingers, or latch onto a remedy like Warne's old guru Richie Benaud, who was introduced to a combination of calamine lotion and boracic powder by a chemist in Timaru. Had he tried it? the chemist asked. It worked wonders on pensioners' leg ulcers. So effective did Benaud find the potion that he shared it with Alf Valentine during the Worrell Trophy of 1960–61, further testifying to the good spirit of that great series.

The riskiest period for any slow bowler is after a lay-off—of exactly the kind Moeen has just returned from. Having always had an ambivalent relationship with his spinning skills, these days he bowls but little. MS Dhoni gave Moeen ten deliveries per game in the recent Indian Premier League; Ben Stokes apportioning him 198 deliveries in Australia's first innings reinforces the Hail Mary nature of his recall. So much for that Ashes 'free hit', as Moeen optimistically called it; Test cricket is only ever a long slog.

In Test cricket, too, everything can be seen as connected, and it is not wisdom after the event to observe that England have here paid a price by opting for batter-keeper Jonny Bairstow over keeper-batter Ben Foakes: plenty of good judges wondered aloud when the decision was made. It has worked out pretty much as one would have expected, if not feared: Bairstow's batting runs have been offset by his semi-regular keeping errors, which narrowed England's lead, have taken critical time out of the game, and also ... added to Moeen's workload.

What if Moeen had struck twice in his fifteenth over, rather than once, and had Cameron Green stumped as well as Travis Head caught? Would his finger have then had time to recover before the more important task of bowling in the fourth innings? Australia's innings would, at any rate, not have been so prolonged that England's openers yesterday found themselves batting in the toughest conditions of the match.

None of these considerations, of course, does cricket measure as meaningfully as it does runs, wickets, and catches, but that does not mean they don't count, and over the course of the Ashes the risk will grow rather than contract. As exciting as Bairstow's batting may be—and it is terrific, chock full of fight and spirit—you would hardly trust him to convey the close-in fielder's helmet from one end to the other safely at the moment.

Things might have been worse for England had rain yesterday not first delayed and then curtailed play for the day with two scoreless batters at the crease after first Duckett and then Crawley offered chances behind the wicket within three deliveries of each other. The crowd suffered these interruptions, it should be said, with commendable forbearance, holding fast to the terraces even as the rain intensified, and showcasing a colourful array of ponchos, anoraks, and, above all, umbrellas. Umbrellas in this country are a serious business. One saw barely two the same.

In Australia, the very thought of rain stirs commentators to dark demands for roofs, canopies, schedule changes, and games to occur on sound stages or in underground caverns, etc. Here, it seems part of the national embrace of discomfort as a way of life. But not every discomfort can just be shrugged off. Just ask unlucky Moeen.

Stumps: England 2nd innings 28/2 (Ollie Pope 0*, Joe Root 0*, 10.3 ov)

19 JUNE

Day 4

The race is not to the swift, nor the battle to the strong, even if you wouldn't routinely bet against either swiftness or strength. Still, in this Test, which has set such a hectic pace, there was something fitting about the fourth afternoon belonging to that epitome of slowness, Nathan Lyon.

At the first drinks break yesterday, the game was converging on the predictable. England having seen off Pat Cummins' virile opening spell, Australia were being attended by their orange-bibbed reserves, Starc, Marsh, Renshaw, and Neser—and what a pleasing anachronism it is that elite cricketers, otherwise so pampered, still cheerfully perform the menial task of waiting on their fellow cricketers.

Root performed running repairs to his helmet while chatting to Cummins; Brook reinserted a sprig under the gaze of umpire Erasmus; and when Erasmus's colleague, Ahsan Raza, turned his back, Lyon moved to the non-striker's end and superstitiously swapped the bails over.

This Lyon likes to do, every now and then, as if to change things up—to reverse the polarities, as it were. I remember him indulging in this habit at Headingley in 2019, when it assuredly did not do the trick. But his first three overs in the morning had

gone for 27, talk was of the timing of England's declaration, and
Australia was searching.

It's at times like these that his captains have often turned
to Lyon, so patient, so phlegmatic, so counter the age, which
rejoices in strike rates as an index of enterprise, almost of virtue:
the scoreboard here gives us runs scored and balls faced, as
though they are the batters' vital signs. Lyon, a common-sense
cricketer who would be at home in any era, seems to get this,
even to harness it.

Asked before the series how he planned to cope with the
psychic challenge of Bazball, Lyon offered up a ready-made
statistic: 'I've been hit for six, it must be getting close to 300
[times] now for me. I'm not worried by it at all, I'm not scared by
it. It provides a chance [of wickets] in my eyes.' It's like the dear,
departed Shane Warne used to say: 'No matter how far they hit
you, it always comes back.'

Two days before the Test, in fact, Lyon asked two of the team's
reserves, Matthew Renshaw and Josh Inglis, to spend an hour in
the nets trying to slog him, just to get used to the sensation. Now,
unobtrusively, unfussily, looking tightly through his sunglasses, in
those creams always as dusty as a janitor's, he went to work.

Joe Root, after a sparkling cameo, got a little greedy, and
threw his head back as he ran past one. Harry Brook, having
bolted to 36 off 27, could only eke 10 from his last 25 before
miscuing a sweep. Lyon grudged 7 from six overs, and Australia
went to lunch in perhaps their best mood of the match.

Afterwards, there was no prising the ball from Lyon's grip,
allowing Cummins to rotate his seamers from the pavilion end,
and affording Australia's captain a degree of control rare for him
in this match. Lyon had no foot marks from old mate Mitchell
Starc to use, but there was his long-time accomplice the DRS
painting a target on front pads.

Lyon duly winkled out Bairstow, just as he was getting going, and Robinson, just as he was getting comfortable. Between times, Lyon rose winded from a superb diving save on the point fence. Nobody gives Australia more on any given day. Lyon's final figures for the match, 53–3–229–8, were swollen by twenty fours and three sixes, but he counted himself coming out ahead, happy to be part of it all. 'It's exciting, to be honest,' he said afterwards in a very mellow press conference. 'I'm bloody proud to be part of it. It's bloody enjoyable.'

By tea, in fact, the Australians had wound the game back to a pace better suited to them. That has been partly the Australians' skill, partly the press of circumstance: a first day of a Test, so securely England's, is the nearest cricket comes to a blank canvas; each succeeding day is then a palimpsest of previous events and growing contexts.

Those with an eye to history were already noting how this game has hugged the contours of the corresponding Test of 2005: from the 407 runs on the first day to the 281-run Australian chase in the fourth innings. That game, of course, Australia lost by 2 runs: you'd hardly rule out a repeat.

England actually made a ragged start to their making-history rhyme, with Anderson conceding 10 in his first over, Broad starting with two no balls, and Bairstow allowing Khawaja's edge to pass him unmolested: his preparedness to dive right does not seem mirrored to the left. So went begging the opportunity to expose Labuschagne on a king pair at one for six. It felt important.

But just when Australia would have felt pleased with their day's work, Broad cast himself as 2023's Flintoff, as excited with his new outswinger as a kid with a new toy in nicking Labuschagne and Steve Smith off in the last half hour, causing Cummins to deploy a nightwatchman at 6.43 pm.

This was another job for which Lyon for years showed willing. This time, he reported, he 'wasn't asked', instead remaining in the dressing room to see Scott Boland's smiling return from a successful mission. One day, Australia will have to find a successor for Lyon with the ball, too. But not yet, thankfully; not quite yet.

Stumps: Australia 2nd innings 107/3 (Usman Khawaja 34*, Scott Boland 13*, 30 ov)

20 JUNE

Day 5

One has been batting poorly for years. The other does not think he can bat. Both had bowled themselves into the ground. Yet there they were, Pat Cummins and Nathan Lyon, at the preposterous hour of 7.00 pm, at the tail end of a tail-end partnership, preparing, with astonishing aplomb, to win a match in which for most of the time Australia had barely clung on.

This fifth day of the Edgbaston Test had for much of its length been the very opposite of the first, when boundaries had cascaded, and a festival atmosphere had prevailed. But its arc was also completing. After multiple meetings of the Bazball executive, Ben Stokes had scattered his field like Cummins on Friday, and Stuart Broad was trying to stir another patriotic roar from the Hollies Stand, albeit with tired arms.

Stokes wanted to attack Lyon, whom he had earlier dropped from a very difficult chance; Lyon was content to be attacked. He was beaten on the outside, twice; he was beaten on the inside, once; between times, he drove a superb boundary. Cummins laced Robinson through the covers, one side of the desperate Pope, the other of the diving Crawley.

Broad next beat Cummins on the inside, but was worked away for a single, whereupon Lyon shovelled over mid-on — a shot of shut-eyed audacity that reduced the target to seven runs. A single reduced the target to a single blow. Cummins almost nicked a bouncer down leg, and barely dug out a yorker from Robinson; facing Broad, Lyon took a lifter on the glove, then bunted a hook, both of which just eluded short leg.

Look, chances are you saw all this, and know what happened, so let me take you back a little in time. The morning had offered comfort only in the prospect of cricket defying our future machine overlords: AI cannot replace men with brooms in English cricket grounds; no algorithm will suffice to sweep rainwater from covers. The scene was a fit subject for LS Lowry or Clarice Beckett, except for the perpetual admonitions on the video screen: show respect, keep hydrating, drink responsibly, use bins, recycle your empties, watch your bags, keep breathing, etc.

The crowd outlasted the inundations, of rain and advice, and settled in at 2.15 pm for a high-spirited day. Except that Australia's approach to their adjusted target of 174 from 77 overs exhibited no compunction about using every last ball, and involved one big investment: in Usman we trust.

Australia's most destructive batters of the last decade had been restricted to 80 runs in six hits in the Test, but their standard-bearer of the last eighteen months was still present, confronted here by the now-traditional fielding chevrons, the standard shuffling between over and around the wicket.

Khawaja, as we know, tackles batting as he tackles life, at a steady pace. But this made the day less of a run chase than a run stalk or even a run creep. Khawaja had lengthy periods becalmed, occasionally guilty of indolence between wickets. His half-century occupied 143 balls, and he was 55 balls in the 30s alone.

The commentators suspected him of that most heinous misdeed, batting without intent, and the Hollies Stand agreed. 'Boring boring Aussies,' rang out the chant. 'Boring boring

Aussies.' Only occasionally, as they drew breath, did one hear a lonely cry of 'Aussie Aussie Aussie, Oi Oi Oi.'

Khawaja's partners came and went—the nightwatchman Boland, the counterpuncher Head, the prodigy Green—but without affecting his pace or his demeanour. His concentration recalled the South African Bruce Mitchell, who, one day in a long innings, looked up at his partner and said: 'When did you come in?' Mitchell had lost track of who he was batting with three wickets earlier.

The grind took its toll on England, too. Fields contracted and spread. Bowlers rested and returned. Moeen looked at his raw finger after every ball, as though trying hard not to think of a pink elephant—the pain of a spinning finger can no more be wished away than that of a toothache.

Pain in the knee hurts also, and Stokes spared his until the 70th over, but struck at once, Khawaja playing a tired shot to the tired cricket ball that stayed a little low. So concluded a microcosm of the contest: Bazball, 666 runs from 866 balls (4.63 runs per over) v Usball 206 from 518 balls (2.38 runs per over). Strike rate bested by work rate.

With the second new ball pending, a gamble by Stokes on the old ball paid off when the fretful Carey offered Root a return catch as he tried to take advantage of the field being up. Then came a counter blast from Cummins, successfully taking that advantage, by heaving two straight sixes. *En garde! Touché!* Remember those forty-two fours and five sixes on Friday? What did they count for now? As observed, neither Cummins nor Lyon had anything like batting form to speak of coming into the match. But they had experience, and the sense, perhaps, of a bigger circle closing.

Four years ago, in the last great Ashes nipper at Headingley, Stokes poached the winning boundary from Cummins, Lyon having shambled in the field. Now Stokes could not gather in Lyon's mis-hook at deep backward square leg, and Cummins ran for his life. At length, as Stokes looked on, Cummins slid a short ball to third man, where overlapping England fielders fumbled the ball into the rope, and the Australian captain charged into Lyon's embrace. So ended a vintage Ashes Test, fit to be ranked with the very best. Where else would you want to be? Seven sleeps till Lord's.

SCOREBOARD

First Test: Birmingham, 16–20 June 2023
England 393/8d & 273

Toss: England
Australia 386 & 282/8

Australia won by 2 wickets

ENGLAND 1ST INNINGS

BATTING		R	B	M	4S	6S	SR
Zak Crawley	c †Carey b Boland	**61**	73	118	7	0	83.56
Ben Duckett	c †Carey b Hazlewood	**12**	10	18	2	0	120.00
Ollie Pope	lbw b Lyon	**31**	44	60	2	0	70.45
Joe Root	not out	**118**	152	269	7	4	77.63
Harry Brook	b Lyon	**32**	37	45	4	0	86.48
Ben Stokes (c)	c †Carey b Hazlewood	**1**	8	6	0	0	12.50
Jonny Bairstow †	st †Carey b Lyon	**78**	78	102	12	0	100.00
Moeen Ali	st †Carey b Lyon	**18**	17	19	2	1	105.88
Stuart Broad	b Green	**16**	21	22	2	0	76.19
Ollie Robinson	not out	**17**	31	30	2	0	54.83
Extras	(lb 6, nb 3)	**9**					
TOTAL	**78 Ov (RR: 5.03)**	**393/8d**					

Did not bat: James Anderson

Fall of wickets: 1-22 (Ben Duckett, 3.4 ov), 2-92 (Ollie Pope, 17.6 ov), 3-124 (Zak Crawley, 26.4 ov), 4-175 (Harry Brook, 37.2 ov), 5-176 (Ben Stokes, 38.4 ov), 6-297 (Jonny Bairstow, 61.4 ov), 7-323 (Moeen Ali, 65.5 ov), 8-350 (Stuart Broad, 70.4 ov)

BOWLING	O	M	R	W	ECON	WD	NB
Pat Cummins	14	0	59	0	4.21	0	0
Josh Hazlewood	15	1	61	2	4.06	0	0
Scott Boland	14	0	86	1	6.14	0	0
Nathan Lyon	29	1	149	4	5.13	0	0
Cameron Green	6	0	32	1	5.33	0	3

AUSTRALIA 1ST INNINGS

BATTING		R	B	M	4S	6S	SR
David Warner	b Broad	9	27	48	2	0	33.33
Usman Khawaja	b Robinson	141	321	478	14	3	43.92
Marnus Labuschagne	c †Bairstow b Broad	0	1	1	0	0	0.00
Steven Smith	lbw b Stokes	16	59	69	0	0	27.11
Travis Head	c Crawley b Ali	50	63	69	8	1	79.36
Cameron Green	b Ali	38	68	85	4	1	55.88
Alex Carey †	b Anderson	66	99	128	10	1	66.66
Pat Cummins (c)	c Stokes b Robinson	38	62	91	0	3	61.29
Nathan Lyon	c Duckett b Robinson	1	6	10	0	0	16.66
Scott Boland	c Pope b Broad	0	5	5	0	0	0.00
Josh Hazlewood	not out	1	1	5	0	0	100.00
Extras	(b 4, lb 6, nb 15, w 1)	26					
TOTAL	116.1 Ov (RR: 3.32)	386					

Fall of wickets: 1-29 (David Warner, 10.1 ov), 2-29 (Marnus Labuschagne, 10.2 ov), 3-67 (Steven Smith, 26.6 ov), 4-148 (Travis Head, 45.3 ov), 5-220 (Cameron Green, 67.1 ov), 6-338 (Alex Carey, 98.4 ov), 7-372 (Usman Khawaja, 112.4 ov), 8-377 (Nathan Lyon, 114.3 ov), 9-378 (Scott Boland, 115.3 ov), 10-386 (Pat Cummins, 116.1 ov)

BOWLING	O	M	R	W	ECON	WD	NB
Stuart Broad	23	4	68	3	2.95	0	7
Ollie Robinson	22.1	5	55	3	2.48	1	1
James Anderson	21	5	53	1	2.52	0	0
Harry Brook	3	1	5	0	1.66	0	1
Moeen Ali	33	4	147	2	4.45	0	0
Ben Stokes	7	0	33	1	4.71	0	6
Joe Root	7	3	15	0	2.14	0	0

ENGLAND 2ND INNINGS

BATTING		R	B	M	4S	6S	SR
Zak Crawley	c †Carey b Boland	7	25	49	0	0	28.00
Ben Duckett	c Green b Cummins	19	28	46	1	0	67.85
Ollie Pope	b Cummins	14	16	42	2	0	87.50
Joe Root	st †Carey b Lyon	46	55	79	5	1	83.63
Harry Brook	c Labuschagne b Lyon	46	52	81	5	0	88.46
Ben Stokes (c)	lbw b Cummins	43	66	115	5	0	65.15
Jonny Bairstow †	lbw b Lyon	20	39	58	3	0	51.28
Moeen Ali	c †Carey b Hazlewood	19	31	42	2	1	61.29
Ollie Robinson	c Green b Lyon	27	44	61	2	0	61.36
Stuart Broad	not out	10	29	51	0	0	34.48
James Anderson	c †Carey b Cummins	12	14	18	2	0	85.71
Extras	(lb 9, nb 1)	10					
TOTAL	**66.2 Ov (RR: 4.11)**	273					

Fall of wickets: 1-27 (Ben Duckett, 8.4 ov), 2-27 (Zak Crawley, 9.1 ov), 3-77 (Ollie Pope, 16.6 ov), 4-129 (Joe Root, 25.1 ov), 5-150 (Harry Brook, 33.4 ov), 6-196(Jonny Bairstow, 45.3 ov), 7-210 (Ben Stokes, 48.2 ov), 8-229 (Moeen Ali, 54.4 ov), 9-256 (Ollie Robinson, 61.5 ov), 10-273 (James Anderson, 66.2 ov)

BOWLING	O	M	R	W	ECON	WD	NB
Pat Cummins	18.2	1	63	4	3.43	0	0
Josh Hazlewood	10	1	48	1	4.80	0	1
Nathan Lyon	24	2	80	4	3.33	0	0
Scott Boland	12	2	61	1	5.08	0	0
Cameron Green	2	0	12	0	6.00	0	0

AUSTRALIA 2ND INNINGS (T: 281 RUNS)

BATTING		R	B	M	4S	6S	SR
Usman Khawaja	b Stokes	65	197	318	7	0	32.99
David Warner	c †Bairstow b Robinson	36	57	75	4	0	63.15
Marnus Labuschagne	c †Bairstow b Broad	13	15	20	3	0	86.66
Steven Smith	c †Bairstow b Broad	6	13	19	1	0	46.15
Scott Boland	c †Bairstow b Broad	20	40	53	2	0	50.00
Travis Head	c Root b Ali	16	24	36	3	0	66.66
Cameron Green	b Robinson	28	66	75	2	0	42.42
Alex Carey †	c & b Root	20	50	63	2	0	40.00
Pat Cummins (c)	not out	44	73	95	4	2	60.27
Nathan Lyon	not out	16	28	62	2	0	57.14
Extras	(lb 10, nb 8)	18					
TOTAL	92.3 Ov (RR: 3.04)	282/8					

Did not bat: Josh Hazlewood

Fall of wickets: 1-61 (David Warner, 17.4 ov), 2-78 (Marnus Labuschagne, 21.3 ov), 3-89 (Steven Smith, 25.3 ov), 4-121 (Scott Boland, 37.2 ov), 5-143 (Travis Head, 44.5 ov), 6-192 (Cameron Green, 63.4 ov), 7-209 (Usman Khawaja, 71.6 ov), 8-227 (Alex Carey, 80.3 ov)

BOWLING	O	M	R	W	ECON	WD	NB
James Anderson	17	1	56	0	3.29	0	1
Stuart Broad	21	3	64	3	3.04	0	4
Ollie Robinson	18.3	7	43	2	2.32	0	3
Moeen Ali	14	2	57	1	4.07	0	0
Joe Root	15	2	43	1	2.86	0	0
Ben Stokes	7	2	9	1	1.28	0	0

21 JUNE

England must stick with Bazball

Victory blesses, and defeat condemns everything in their vicinity. Before the First Test, Bazball was regarded by the English as a guarantor of success; now, at least by Australian lights, it has been utterly discredited. Bring out your buzzwords. We will soon cut them down to size.

This is almost certainly the wrong conclusion to draw from Edgbaston's wonderful Test. For a start, the cricket was more nuanced than bash v block. After the first day, there were periods where England batted with care and bowled restrictively; there was Australian thrust as well as parry. England certainly played with the greater flair; England also made many more mistakes.

They squandered half-a-dozen catches, to Australia's one; they bowled 23 no balls, to Australia's four. In doing so, they missed opportunities to cut man-of-the-match Usman Khawaja short in each innings. Australia became the World Test Champion partly by punishing error more reliably than any other country, and did it again.

But, and this is the important part, England ran Australia as close as any team has in the last two years in anything other than low-bouncing, spin-friendly conditions. They also put in their most uniformly good Ashes performance in eight years: the two

Tests England have won against Australia since 2015 were (a) one man's handiwork after a first innings slump for 67 and (b) a dead rubber when they were gifted first innings on a flat pitch.

So, far from being discredited, Bazball is already a success, having hugely narrowed the yawning gap between the teams in the 2021–22 Ashes. Play on, Stokesy! To paraphrase Trent Crim, if Bazball is wrong, it's hard to imagine being right. Australia needed all their knowhow and sagacity to come out ahead. The same will apply in the next four Tests.

Where Bazball needs modification is, rather, in the matter of detail. Stokes and McCullum are right to see a fine line between promoting climates of excellence and of fear, and how a punitive zero tolerance of error can undermine confidence and promote inhibition.

But there remain minimums that need to be striven for, and freedom should not excuse the kind of sloppiness that pervaded England's cricket in Birmingham: problems of fielding and of overstepping the front line are not to be addressed by friendly pints and feel-good golf. Getting that balance right is the approach's next step.

What is seriously absurd is that at the end of one of the best Test matches in memory, both Australia and England were docked significant monies and WTC points for slow over rates: England ended up with negative two points. And the question must be: *Cui bono?*

Slow over-rate penalties, then enforced by fines, came into the game thirty years ago at a time when there were well-founded fears about the future of slow bowling, thanks to the influence of the four-member West Indies' attacks. They were consolidated by the demands of television to guarantee a minimum of content in the entertainment package.

They have lingered into an era where neither are sources

of major concern: there were 112 overs of spin at Edgbaston and huge audiences. So why the penalties? It is surely wrong that sub-par over rates are penalised by the WTC, whereas sub-standard surfaces — a far greater blight — are not, instead incurring meaningless sanctions against individual venues that do nothing to discourage the practice of tailored pitch preparation. If an overs minimum is something to aim for, it should be the responsibility of the on-field umpires, who already have powers to penalise time-wasting under Law 41.9.2.

The problem with the existing law is that it imagines time-wasting to be the prerogative of fielding teams, where anyone who watches international cricket these days knows that the most tiresome aspect of Test cricket is the batters' endless traffic in drinks, gloves, helmets, tape, towels, defibrillators, complete Meccano sets, etc, conveyed to and from the boundary line by orange-bibbed minions and officious medicos.

The law needs to reflect reality. If Steve Smith sweats so copiously that he needs fresh gloves every ten runs or so, then he needs to see a doctor rather than use the twelfth man as his valet. If players need more general relief, they should be capable of waiting until the game's ample intervals, which are only an hour apart, after all.

On the last day at Edgbaston, two reserve players brought a drink and towel out for Usman Khawaja ten minutes before tea. Ten minutes! FOMO caused Cameron Green, who had just come to the wicket, to join them. The fielders looked on listlessly; the umpires did nothing to speed them up. One of these days, a player will get a pedicure, and nobody will bat an eyelid.

In recent years, the trend has been to the diminution of on-field umpiring responsibilities. Lately, for example, they have been relieved of supervision of the front line, and even lost the vestigial authority of the soft signal. It's time to reverse that trend by empowering umpires to supervise comings and goings on the field more closely, maybe even to seal the boundaries at the start of every session. In the event of extreme heat, the game already provides for an additional drinks break; but the trend to miscellaneous interruption must otherwise cease. Parched mouth? Sweaty palms? Suck it up: you're an elite athlete.

At the same time, that the only points penalties levied in the World Test Championship is for over rates is perfectly disproportionate. Failure to bowl a minimum of deliveries is, at worst, a third-order offence. Nobody at Edgbaston felt remotely short-changed, yet England ended up worse off than if the entire game had been washed out. So there's a take on the First Test. Bazball is underestimated, and over rates are … overrated.

26 JUNE
NATHAN LYON

Spin to win

You come at the king, Omar Little warned us in *The Wire*, you best not miss. Will England rue their failure to polish Australia's tail off at Edgbaston?

Ben Stokes' team are straining to persuade us otherwise, having, curiously, deemed the First Test as good as a win—a species of denialism in the 'alternative facts' category, even more ambitious than retrospectively declaring the 2021–22 Ashes not to have counted.

It's true that the score line should in all fairness be closer to 0.55 v 0.45 rather than 1 v 0. But the reality of the latter cannot be waved away, any more than Rory McIlroy can wish away that single stroke fewer of Wyndham Clark's: England must now win a minimum of two matches against Australia while preventing them from winning any more.

It is not so long since Steve Smith and Marnus Labuschagne both failed in a Test—they were kept to 62 in four hits at Delhi earlier this year. But they never both failed in each innings of consecutive Tests, which suggests an opportunity forgone by

England at Edgbaston, and a good omen for Australia at Lord's.

What gaped in Birmingham and threatens to yawn indefinitely, furthermore, is Australia's slow-bowling advantage, encapsulated by Lord's hosting Nathan Lyon's hundredth consecutive Test, and the doubt about Moeen Ali playing consecutive Tests.

No one has needed to worry whether the tourists' thirty-five-year-old off-spinner will be fit; nobody has ever expressed concern about his loads; he is the banker's banker, the maid of all work, his lifetime's economy (conceding less than three an over) now matched by a new penetration (79 wickets at 24 in Australia's last fifteen Tests).

Filling the gaps and providing the respite, unfazed by reverse sweeps and ramps, routinely stepping backwards to his bowling mark as if to maintain total engagement in his task, he makes the whole Australian mechanism tick. A bowling average of less than 25 in 65 Test wins shows how integral Lyon has been to their success. A first-class system that provides Darren Stevens with a livelihood till the age of forty-six but in a decade has failed to advance a successor to Graeme Swann, meanwhile, is surely not fit for purpose. But you knew that already.

Although nobody will make a biopic about Lyon, he has in some ways been as remarkable as his eminent predecessor Shane Warne. Warne had played seven first-class matches before his Test debut; Lyon had played five. When Warne came along, Australia were looking for a new spinner; when Lyon came along, they were in search of a new Warne.

Like Warne, too, Lyon has remained his own man, standing aslant the game's trends. Not only has Australia historically been far friendlier to wrist-spin than finger-spin, but a decade or so ago the demise of the latter was freely prophesied. In the future, it was argued, orthodox finger spin would not suffice. Practitioners would need either a variety of deliveries, including a doosra and/or carrom ball turning away from the right-hander, or the talent to bat at six or seven, with counterpunching capacity. Ravi Ashwin fulfilled the former prediction, Ravi Jadeja the latter, while Ashton Agar began Australia's experimentation along similar lines — and ended it.

For Lyon ploughed on, unadorned and unreconstructed: a good fielder, a competent tailender, and a solid citizen, but with the ball the acme of orthodoxy. Mystery spinner? In mystery terms, he is more Agatha Christie than Patricia Highsmith. But Poirot still packs them in.

Perhaps because his gifts are so conventional, Lyon has been, at times, a little prone both to self-doubt and to overcorrection — when ten years ago he announced that Australia would 'definitely be looking to end a few careers' in a home Ashes, it sounded like the worst kind of sports-psych ventriloquism.

These days, Lyon is more commonly reflective, sometimes wry. Asked at Edgbaston about a day of listening to the Barmy Army's chorus of 'You're a shit Mooen Ali', he expressed warm appreciation of the crowd's enthusiasm, but they didn't seem to like Moeen very much, did they? Boom-tish.

England will be primed to attack Lyon at Lord's, as they did at Edgbaston, understanding his stabilising role in Australia's bowling stratagems. It will be instructive to see if the ground's boundary ropes are in as far as they were during the recent Ireland Test, when the playing surface looked only slightly bigger than that for a table-top Test match game.

But if Lord's lives up to its reputation for bland, featureless pitches, and the sun continues beating down, Lyon will be short odds to claim the five scalps he needs to reach 500 Test wickets, if only because nobody will churn through more overs.

You seldom, moreover, get the better of Lyon for long. Kept

to a solitary wicket at Nagpur during the recent Border-Gavaskar Trophy, he claimed eighteen wickets in the next two Tests. At Edgbaston, he was clocked for three sixes, and had three batters stumped. He will take that ratio any time. Come at this king, you best not miss either.

27 JUNE

THE ASHES TRADITION

Expletives deleted

Zak Crawley expects England to win the Lord's Test by, 'I don't know, 150 runs.' Ollie Robinson has expressed surprise that Australia were 'reluctant to go toe-to-toe with us' at Edgbaston.

For the latter and various other temerities, Matthew Hayden has deemed Robinson an 'ordinary cricketer', Justin Langer predicted he will be 'ripped apart', and Michael Clarke opined that he should be 'back playing clubbies'. Oh, and Jim Maxwell thinks Jonny Bairstow is 'overweight' and 'not a wicketkeeper'.

I could go on, but you get the idea. As much a part of the soundscape of an Ashes summer as willow on leather is the mutual baiting and back chat of the rival camps. Perhaps it is a little riper than usual, given the *kulturkampf* of Bazball v CumonAussie. But in a game where the wait is almost as much a part as the play, this cheerily contained antagonism is what we live for.

And maybe, just maybe, we could do with cherishing it a little more, given the backdrop of yesterday's release of the scathing Independent Commission for Equity in Cricket, which has reported the game to be 'rife with racism, sexism and elitism'.

The conclusions can hardly surprise many. Sexism and elitism in a country where three of fifty-seven prime ministers have been female, and forty-four have come from two universities? Who knew? The shock would surely be if cricket were found to be a rainbow-hued, classless, and colourblind utopia within the nation.

The only plea to be made in mitigation is to wonder how well any cricket nation would fare under such unsparing analysis. Not only has Australia promoted just two Indigenous male cricketers in its history, but India has selected only four Dalits, and Sri Lanka not a dozen Tamils. And while there are greater grounds for optimism about women's cricket than ever, the base remains way low.

Be that as it may, England and Australia will take the field at Lord's today in a spirit at odds with the frequent lamentation that 'You can't say anything anymore'—because, where the Ashes is concerned, frankly, you can.

What Australia's longest-serving prime minister, Sir Robert Menzies, said sixty years ago remains true, that the length and strength of the rivals' cultural connections provide a licence for their disinhibited relations.

'Great Britain and Australia are of the same blood and allegiance and history and instinctive mental processes,' said Menzies. 'We know each other so well that, thank heaven, we don't have to be too tactful with each other.'

They can even, at times, borrow from one another. Ollie Robinson, of course, was quick to excuse his Edgbaston expletives by reference to Ricky Ponting; there should be a prize for the first Aussie to invoke Joe Root in the context of their own reverse ramp.

English crowds have grown as boisterous and partisan as their Australian counterparts, and Australian cricket administrators have been quick to co-opt English innovations, from the six-ball over to one-day and T20 formats. So many administrators are here at the moment, in fact, that there can hardly be so much as a club secretary left down under.

So how have Anglo-Australian cricket relations managed to remain so robust in an environment of worsening anxiety about giving offence? Cultural and ethnic similarities certainly help. But while India and Pakistan have millennia of shared history, in cricket terms they seem barely able to stand the sight of each other.

It's not like there aren't sensitivities either. When Ponting bristled about Robinson the other day, one was reminded of the remarks of a notable observer of antipodean cultural mores, who said that 'the Australian, while impatient of criticism from without, is not given to criticising either himself or his country …'

There may be something in sentiments uttered by Menzies' great prime ministerial peer and rival, John Curtin, in a speech at Mansion House on his only visit to England in May 1944, and reported with approval in Wisden the following year.

The lines, often quoted, have a pleasing ring but an underestimated subtlety, in the way they balance the very important and the apparently trivial: 'Lord's and its traditions belong to Australia just as much as England. We are defending the City of London and those 22 yards of turf which we hope will be used time and time again, so that the Motherland and Australia can decide whether the six-ball over is better than the eight-ball over.'

It seems to me that this goes to the very heart of the Ashes' appeal — the relishable freedom to treat what's ultimately quite unimportant as a matter of life and death. Lots of things these days come with an importance that is irresistible, embedded, and exhausting; the Ashes' significance is uncoerced, simulated, playful, our own creation.

It's incarnate in the quasi-religious regard for a 10.5cm, 22g terracotta urn originally designed for a woman's perfume; it's in every story that listeners to *Cricket Et Cetera* have shared with us following the climax of the First Test, from a father on a family holiday near Uluru who stood for hours in the freezing darkness with a satellite dish so his ten-year-old could hear the commentary, to an Englishman in Connecticut who timed his walk from a conference call to a school pick-up perfectly to allow the *Cricinfo* app to refresh.

Perhaps, most of all, is it in every huff and puff of rival players and fans in the Ashes tradition, generally on the brink of permissible rudeness, but with a laugh blessedly never too far away, and a pleasure in the ease of pushing each other's buttons. You might be wondering, for instance, about that shrewd observation, quoted above, of Australian prickliness where criticism is concerned. Donald Horne? Barry Humphries? Nope: Douglas Jardine.

The Second Test:
Lord's

28 June–3 July 2023
Australia won by 43 runs

MATCH REPORT

Lord's a-leaping

To the last ball of the 52nd over of England's second innings in the Second Test, Jonny Bairstow shouldered arms, looked reflexively down, and then commenced to wander off down the pitch. His Australian counterpart, Alex Carey, had in the meantime lobbed the ball back towards the stumps. What happened next will entwine the 2023 Ashes, these individuals, Australia, and England ever more. Hearing the stumps broken, Bairstow looked around in horror, though not perhaps surprise. He had tried the same ploy at Edgbaston, hopeful of catching Marnus Labuschagne unawares; now was the biter bit. For all the later posturing about the body language of the respective umpires, Chris Gaffaney and Ahsan Raza, they had not called 'over': there was really no necessity for a referral to the third umpire, Marais Erasmus, who quickly confirmed that the requirements of Law 20.1.2 had been met, and Bairstow was stumped.

Back he walked into a Lord's pavilion that commenced to boil like a kettle of annoyance; by the time the Australians walked through it on the way to lunch five overs later, it was whistling with indignation. Cummins and his men were followed through the hallowed precincts of the Long Room and up the stairs by hissings of 'cheat' from a host of blazered buffoons; already the

Australians were being pilloried on radio talkback and assailed by outrage queens. Worse still, later that afternoon, even more unforgivably, they won.

This covfefe, one suspects, England rather welcomed, as it pasted over manifest flaws in their performance. Stokes won the toss and sent Australia in, only to see them pile up five for 339 on the first day on a slow surface against some lacklustre bowling from a lopsided attack, England having left out their solitary spinner, Moeen Ali, in favour of the young seamer Josh Tongue. Refreshed by a fallow week, Steve Smith touched something like his best, putting on 102 (155 balls) with Marnus Labuschagne and 118 (122 balls) with Travis Head. Neither Broad nor Robinson threatened; the ball followed Anderson in the field, but shunned the stumps and the edge when he bowled. Tongue was, in the end, probably the pick of the bowlers. The solitary decisive act was Bairstow's removal of a Stop Oil Now protester, whom he picked up and carried off like a removalist hefting a piece of unattractive furniture; the protester's gesture of triumph through this added a suitable flourish of the ludicrous.

At one for 180 after tea on the second day, England looked to be making the most of the benign conditions also, and if they had but known were on the brink of a vital moment in the series. Taking on the succession of Australian bouncers, Ben Duckett top-edged Cameron Green to deep backward square leg, where Nathan Lyon pulled up in advance of the descending ball. He crumpled, and came up sore, before hobbling off with the physiotherapist; the gravity of his injury was momentarily obscured by some overexcited batting in which England lost three for 32, all to the short ball, in 44 balls, and then five for 46 in fifteen overs before lunch the following morning to concede a 91-run deficit. Nor could they make use of favourable bowling conditions to bowl the rest of that third day, through which Khawaja diligently guarded and deflected.

On the fourth morning, England frustratedly resorted to Bazbounce: rather at odds with their evangel about saving Test cricket, as it was hardly likely to endear the game to anyone, but successful. In the teeth of short ball after short ball, Khawaja, Smith, Head, Green, Carey, Cummins, and Hazlewood all fell either hooking or fending. Australia lost eight for 92 in fifty austere overs to Broad, Tongue, Robinson, and Stokes; Anderson, whose game this is not, looked something of a wallflower. Australia's concern for England's capacity for chasing was reflected in a brief, painful cameo by the luckless Lyon, propped in the saddle like El Cid. He was warmly received by England's fielders and fans—rather a contrast to the following day's shenanigans—perhaps partly because his appearance clarified that he would be unable to bowl.

England made a poor start on their fourth-innings target of 371, with Starc removing Crawley and Pope in consecutive overs, and Cummins disposing of Root and Brook in the same over. But while Stokes remained, despair was impossible, and with the end in sight, Duckett had a stroke of good fortune, deflecting Hazlewood to fine leg in the act of evading, where Starc took a good running catch that, in falling to his knees, he unaccountably dashed on the ground. Though Australians were irked, the umpires correctly applied the letter of Law 33.3 ('The act of making a catch shall start from the time when the ball first comes into contact with a fielder's person and shall end when a fielder obtains complete control over both the ball and his/her own movement'), and England entered the last day needing 257 from its last six wickets: difficult, but, after their chasing feats the previous year, not inconceivable against an attack sans its spinner.

Their prospects waxed in the first hour of the final day, when Duckett and Stokes knocked 60 off that target without running obvious risks. The odds lengthened when Duckett top-edged a hook at Hazlewood, Carey subtly positioning himself to leg for the set play, and Bairstow made his fatal wandering, Carey again alert and proactive—if not in the eyes of the obnoxious bigots of the Marylebone membership.

The one positive to emerge from Bairstow's reaction was Stokes' equal and opposite reaction. He was at the time 61 off 126 balls. Cummins brought himself back to pepper Broad, who nonetheless held firm, and wrung every ounce of melodrama from the affair by conspicuously checking on when and if the ball was dead; Stokes acted like he wanted to remove the question altogether by killing the ball for good. He almost took Cummins' hand off with a caught-and-bowled chance. Then, with three consecutive sixes from Green, launched in the direction of the shorter boundary on the Mound and Tavern side, Stokes barged to a century, which he greeted with familiar impassivity—familiar, at any rate, to anyone who had been at Headingley in 2019.

The flashbacks kept coming. Hazlewood resumed after lunch, was launched over long on, and top-edged to fine leg, where a clammy-handed Smith dropped the catch. In the bowler's next over, he found himself punched over square leg and launched over long leg. Hazlewood gave way to Starc, who was taken for sixes behind and in front of square leg. Just then, a statement dropped from Cricket Australia: 'Australian management has requested the Marylebone Cricket Club (MCC) investigate several incidents involving spectators in the members area during lunch on day five of the Lord's Test. It is alleged players and staff from the Australian team were verbally abused, with some being physically contacted, as they made their way to lunch through the members area.' Alarming as this was, the abuse and contact of Stokes' bat was Australia's priority during an impromptu consultation between Cummins, Smith, Warner, Khawaja, and Labuschagne at the pavilion end.

This brains trust decided on a new policy of width from around the wicket, implemented first by Green and then Starc. The effect was marked. Anxious to keep the strike, Stokes reined himself in. When Hazlewood was reintroduced after drinks, England's captain threw his hands at a short ball, aiming for the longer boundary, only for the top edge to loop to Carey jogging towards backward point: kept to scoring only seven runs from his last 38 deliveries, Stokes had finally lost the staring contest. Robinson fell limply, and Broad bravely, both caught at fine leg. And, after a swing or two, Tongue had his leg stump removed by Starc. At the presentation, Stokes was cheered to the echo; Cummins and man-of-the-match Smith were loudly booed.

Afterwards, Stokes conceded that the umpires had been correct, but said that in the same position he would not have appealed: 'I am not disputing the fact it is out because it is out. If the shoe was on the other foot, I would have put more pressure on the umpires and asked whether they had called over and had a deep think about the whole spirit of the game and would I want to do something like that. For Australia it was the match-winning moment. Would I want to win a game in that manner? The answer for me is no.' Nobody asked if he would be requesting Bairstow to desist from the same practice, or even how six bouncers an over could be accommodated in the spirit of cricket.

Asked if it would affect relations between the team, coach Brendon McCullum was non-committal: 'I can't imagine we'll be having a beer anytime soon, if that's what you're asking.'

Cummins found this odd, 'given how Baz likes a beer', and was succinctly unrepentant: 'I thought it was totally fair play. That's how the rule is. Some people might disagree.' And they did. My word, they did.

28 JUNE

Day 1

Steve Smith paused. This — a cricketer who is a blur of mannerisms and always seems busy doing something — he does not often do. But on the boundary rope at Lord's, as he prepared to step on the field after lunch yesterday, Australia's premier batter visibly stopped, stood on the spot, took time, took stock, and took a deep breath. His shoulders rose and fell; he looked up, around, and stretched at the waist.

There were a few dim-bulb boos as he continued on his way: there are, in England, always some. It was a key moment in the contest, Australia having lost its openers either side of lunch; it was a key moment also for Smith, who had scrounged and scavenged his few runs at Edgbaston, for even batters as great as he is live a little on their nerves. Marnus Labuschagne was 5 off 22 balls, almost as though he didn't want to get started without his friend and familiar, like a diner reluctant to order before their companion arrived. Smith was not in a hurry, but nor was he waiting.

The surface held few terrors. No Jofra Archer awaited Smith this time. Instead, he punched a floaty half-volley down the ground for 3, nailed a pull shot and then a couple of cover drives, and within a quarter of an hour the game had a new complexion. The previously becalmed Labuschagne got moving, driving Broad precisely through the covers, and flicking away some generous leg stump half-volleys. Between times, there was the communication, the seemingly madcap gesturing that is this pair's personal semaphore, providing each other with real-time data on the bowlers, the pitch, their respective states of mind, their pleasure in each other's company, etc.

It proved, largely, Australia's day, despite England's efforts at the toss to seize the initiative in overcast conditions, and despite two wickets against the run of play after 6.00 pm. Smith remained in harness at the end, his 9000th Test run behind him, his thirty-second Test hundred beckoning, his average again past 60.

The lights blazed throughout, and there were multiple interruptions, including catching practice for Jonny Bairstow with a protester soon after the start. Fortunately, Bairstow was not required to dive to his left, as he again failed to do when Khawaja (on 1) edged Anderson, replaying the first over of the second innings at Edgbaston — the chance to Root went begging.

The pitch proved a sheep in wolf's clothing, offering minimal seam movement, little pace, and lacklustre carry. Broad's first delivery, delivered at a gentle 77.1 mph, bounced thrice on the way to the keeper. There was, at least, swing in the air, and slant from the slope. Warner was beaten, semi-regularly, but usually managed to keep his defensive shape, and when he did not was dropped by the unreliable Pope at fourth slip, so avoiding a sixteenth dismissal by Broad.

Warner's 66 was a busy innings — if not skittish, then certainly fizzy with ideas, moving this way and that around the crease, fetching offside balls to leg, standing forward of his ground, but seizing quickly on the short ball. Taking singles, he still explodes like a sprinter from the blocks; coming back for second and third runs, he is so swift he appears always to be running downhill.

As noon approached, so did Josh Tongue — another of those monosyllabic names, along with Broad, Brook, and Root, that invests England's team sheet with such a wholesome earthiness that you hanker for Wood and Stone, and fantasise of cricketers called Field and Wild. From over the wicket, Tongue started wide to the off and short on leg, and was dobbed for six as Warner reached his half-century. But he settled in around the wicket, and posed problems with the incline before Smith and Labuschagne combined for their ninth hundred partnership.

England were tighter after tea, but the ball was softer, the light better, and Travis Head there to do Travis Head things — to punch straight, to plink to leg, to prey on width, and to help add 50 in 52 balls. Smith played his best shot, an imperious straight drive from Tongue to go to 61; in the same over, Head played his, a muscular pull, that raised his 50 in 48 balls. Just after 6.00 pm, however, Head lost his, charging Root, and Green miscued to mid-off.

England hardly deserved their late break. Their bowling effort had little zest, meagre entertainment value, and was certainly not going to save Test cricket. Broad was down on pace. Robinson seems always to be starting up, like a car in cold weather. Pope left the field nursing his shoulder. Thirteen byes were conceded, and twelve no balls bowled, making thirty-five for the series. That's not Bazball; that's Badball.

Most worrying must be two of England's most storied names. Anderson now has one for 138 in the series, and the body language to match. Stokes also looks ginger and not in a good way, jogging in, uncertain around the front line, hardly following through, shaking his head ruefully as he walks back.

Just before tea, Labuschagne drove, not hard but hard enough, down the ground, towards the pavilion. Anderson and Stokes set off gamely in pursuit, but hardly moved much faster than the

hovercraft covers, and the ball comfortably beat them to the rope.
Having started this series with such gleeful abandon, England
spent most of their day likewise, in panting pursuit. They, too,
must pause, to reflect.

Stumps: Australia 1st innings 339/5 (Steven Smith 85, Alex Carey
11*, 83 ov)*

29 JUNE

Day 2

Autocorrect on my laptop has a habit of turning 'Bazball' into 'baseball'. It's been irritating me all summer. But after tea at Lord's yesterday, it started to look predictive.

Between lunch and tea, in the absence of any seam movement, Australia's attack had searched for swing, with little success, and allowed themselves to be picked off, to the extent of England accumulating one for 188 in 38 overs.

At the second interval, Pat Cummins' bullpen changed tack: it was time to dispense with slips, gullies, and good lengths; to explore the middle of the pitch, and the potential of verticality to induce error.

So, for a confounding hour, there we were: one of Australia's finest fast-bowling trios straining to get the ball above eye level; Cameron Green pounding the ball in so short he was almost bowling yorkers to himself, and only hazily aware of the front line between times; and England, once bitten but never shy, pointing to the fences.

It didn't go well for the hosts; it might have gone worse. Three set batters popped up ugly foul balls. After a dozen overs of the stuff, England would have been five for 243, in pursuit of 416 with a long tail, had Harry Brook's line drive/pull shot not burst through Marnus Labuschagne's hands at square leg.

Yet perhaps as significant was the collateral damage that Australia sustained when, scrambling for a top edge from Duckett, Lyon injured a calf. If the medical prognosis is as discouraging as the immediate naked-eye verdict, Lyon's remarkable 100-Test marathon is in jeopardy. No scans are scheduled, but watch this space.

Of the day's first two-thirds, the hosts had much the better. In the morning, Steve Smith breezed through the 80s and 90s to an eighth Test hundred in England, then reacted to his dismissal for 110 as though he had received news of a family bereavement. He wasn't wrong either: runs unmade on this surface may prove as costly as those conceded.

Getting the band back together, meanwhile, is an idea with instinctive appeal and mixed dividends. When Australia reconstituted for Lord's the attacks that had won them Ashes Tests at home and away, plus much more besides, there was an immediate pang of name recognition and continuity. Starc, Hazlewood, Cummins, Lyon: these have been Australia's first choice for most of the last eight years, the occasional injury and lateral thought apart.

These conditions—a Lord's pitch so weary, stale, flat, and unprofitable for bowlers, set in a square too lush for reverse—may not be the best place to make a judgement. But in the afternoon the reunion looked like a promoter's brainstorm gone wrong. Fields languished. Figures distended. Cummins searched for inspiration; spectators reached for more champagne.

Ben Duckett and Zak Crawley laid out a non-baseball Bazball—speed without haste, purpose without flamboyance, demanding a deep point that cost Australia a third slip to the pacemen and an extra fielder near the bat for spin, allowing singles that accentuated the contrast of short, stocky, left-handed

Welcome to Bazball: Zak Crawley, with old-fashioned class (above), and Joe Root, with new-fashioned flair (below), introduce Australia to English batting in the Stokes-McCullum era on the opening day of the First Test at Edgbaston.
Ryan Pierse/Getty Images

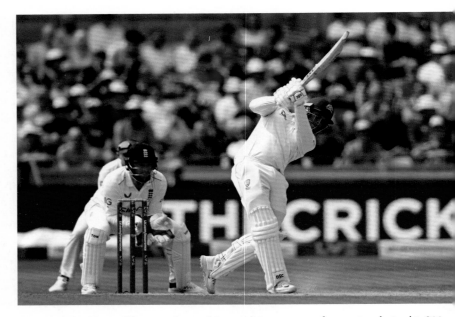

Usman Apart: Usman Khawaja takes on Moeen Ali in a rare act of aggression during his 800-minute vigil in the First Test (above), where he was man of the match for his 141 and 65.
Shaun Botterill/Getty Images

We Have Lift-off: Pat Cummins hoists Nathan Lyon (above left) after their 55-run ninth-wicket partnership carried Australia to a stirring victory at Edgbaston; Jonny Bairstow fills in for security (above right) after the first morning at Lord's is interrupted by a Just Stop Oil protest.
Stu Forster/Getty Images

Letting Go: David Warner (above left) and Travis Head (above right) take divergent approaches to an overcast beginning of the Second Test at Lord's, before Pat Cummins seals the deal for Australia on the fourth evening in a telling spell, bowling Harry Brook (below).
Philip Brown, Stu Forster, Adam Davy/Getty Images

My Way: Nobody does cricket quite like Steve Smith. His 110 and 34 at Lord's, full of unique flourishes, won him the man-of-the-match award (above); he was quick to commiserate with Ben Stokes, whose 155 had almost seized the game and the medal (below).

Ryan Pierse, Stu Forster/Getty Images

Wood Chop: With the inclusion for the Third Test at Headingley of Mark Wood (above), England gained a new speed and spirit; when he beat the previously unhurried Khawaja for pace on the first morning (below), the effect was immediate.

Richard Heathcote, Stu Forster/Getty Images

The Comeback Kids: Mitch Marsh's 118 in the Third Test was the most authoritative Australian batting of the 2023 Ashes (above), but nineteen wickets at 18 in the last three Tests made Chris Woakes a well-deserved Compton-Miller Medallist.

Stu Forster, Philip Brown/Getty Images

Batting in Two Moods: Both batting four-and-a-half hours, the centurions in the Fourth Test at Old Trafford showed Test cricket in all its shades. Zak Crawley rode his luck in a barnstorming 189 (above); Marnus Labuschagne kept his cool in a studious 111 (below).
Alex Davidson, Stu Forster/Getty Images

Come Back Jonny: Barely a backstop when the Ashes began, Jonny Bairstow batted and kept well in the last two Tests, with no better moment than this limber catch (above) of Mitch Marsh off Moeen Ali on the last day of the Fifth Test at The Oval.

Ryan Pierse/Getty Images

Close Your Eyes and Think of England: Ben Stokes anguishes over dropping Steve Smith (above left) before Stuart Broad and Joe Root celebrate the penultimate Australian wicket (above right) as the Ashes converges on a two-all scoreline.

Stu Forster, Philip Brown/Getty Images

Duckett and long, tall, right-handed Crawley. The crowd popped corks uninterruptedly.

Just as the first-wicket partnership assumed threatening proportions, Crawley rather lurched down the pitch to Lyon, and Alex Carey made a third difficult stumping this series look easy. Carey, who soon after dived down the leg side to take a fullish in-ducker from Cummins that almost yorked Ollie Pope, had another unobtrusively excellent day behind the stumps, unlucky to be debited with two lots of four byes as Green and Starc lost direction.

So to Australia's post-tea escapades, whose qualified success implies that we are likely to see them again. Duckett fell two runs short of a century he deserved; Pope wasted a start, and Root a no-ball reprieve. Two excellent catches were taken by the incomparable Smith, and another by the versatile Warner, but Australia may rue Labuschagne's mistake: with 45 off 51 balls, Harry Brook is set for the morrow.

Such strategies, too, are necessarily a temporary expedient: sustained short bowling is hard yakka for pace bowlers. And as the visitors' impetus ran out, and Ben Stokes exercised a calming influence, Cummins had to rely on Head in Lyon's stead, and then even an over of rough-and-ready round-armers from Smith. Nine wickets for 355 in a day's play. Bazball? Baseball? Better.

Stumps: England 1st innings 278/4 (Harry Brook 45*, Ben Stokes 17*, 61 ov)

30 JUNE

Day 3

Sporting quotations seldom age well. Nor are they designed to. But an observation from Marnus Labuschagne, on the eve of this Lord's Test, has taken only a few days to come into its prime.

Asked to reflect on Joe Root's bravura batting at Birmingham, Australia's number three reflected that England's adherence to the creed of attack cut both ways: 'That's the benefit for us with the way that they're playing.

'They're playing aggressive cricket, he's doing it in a different method, which is great, but it brings opportunities for us. Hopefully at some part of the series, that will pay off.' That was Monday; come Friday it was jackpot time.

Pat Cummins' Australians had sensed the prospect after tea on Thursday, when England's top order batted as if mindful of an imminent tee time. Now the bowlers threw down another short-ball gauntlet, with a deep-set field designed to absorb its being picked up.

They needed this ploy to work, too. Although official word from the Australian camp is that Nathan Lyon will feature in this game as needed, said camp is notoriously opaque: news could be withheld of a player having their leg amputated, on grounds of lack of clarity about whether the leg might not be growing back.

So Cummins was really restricted to two other specialist bowlers, whom England could, potentially, grind down, ahead of both a second innings and another Test starting in less than a week.

So if ever a Test match occasion cried out for a speck of a smidgen of a soupçon of restraint, this was it. One wicketless hour, and Lyon might have been warming up in a moon boot. But after Mitchell Starc removed Ben Stokes with a swift delivery into the armpit, the rest followed, not so much bullishly as naively.

Harry Brook has probably guaranteed he will not get another ball in his half this summer; Jonny Bairstow exhibited all the patience of a child at a fairground; and Ollie Robinson, he of the 'three number XIs', batted like one of four, running down the wicket to Green and then to Head.

Stuart Broad perished in the same over, and instead of Australia's bowlers being denied respite, it was England's, including its forty-year-old figurehead, back on duty less than twenty-four hours after a 100-over first innings. Did it 'feel' to England like they had a first innings lead, as it felt to them like they won at Birmingham? It should not have: this cricket was careless, not carefree, with a touch of arrogance, too.

To be fair, yesterday's conditions at Lord's were not straightforward for batting. One had to be prepared to battle. David Warner was—his second innings was hardly the Lord's sign-off he'd have hoped for. The day was chill, the light dim. He misread; he mistimed; he missed. He left a lot of balls, but was denied the width to free his arms; he top-edged a short delivery into space on the leg side.

An hour after lunch, Usman Khawaja also played at three balls in a row from Robinson, each narrowly beating the edge as they seamed away with the batter declining to follow. From the non-striker's end, Warner flashed him a thumbs-up. Australia's lead was already 138, and things were coming up roses in the Harris Garden.

By the time Warner was declined a second reprieve by the third umpire, he had spared his colleagues two testing hours in the middle: his 25 was the kind of contribution, numerically insignificant, that goes to the winning of Test matches.

Khawaja, as ever, was laid back to the point of virtual recumbency. Bowling to him in this mood must feel like hurling a ball as hard as you can into a mattress. Even his boundaries accrue subtly. Two through the off side off Broad were almost soundless, leaned into late. He stroked so gently up the slope that one half-expected the ball to roll back.

Khawaja's single stroke of violence, a pull shot from Tongue, should have been caught at mid-wicket by Anderson: the third time in four innings that England have offered him the second chance he hardly needs. The home team's out-cricket, in fact, was again scrappy.

Although he has had a better match here than at Birmingham, Bairstow conceded four byes down the leg side by making no gesture to stop the ball: he simply fell over like a boy pretending to be shot in a game of cowboys and Indians. Nor did he press for England to review Broad's lbw appeal against Labuschagne off Broad, even if this did not cost his team too many. But Australia had already seized the opportunity that mattered. They will not readily give it back.

Stumps: Australia 2nd innings 130/2 (Usman Khawaja 58*, Steven Smith 6*, 45.4 ov)

1 JULY

Day 4

Surely not. Surely, surely not. Mitchell Starc thought as much. No sooner had Australia's ninth wicket fallen yesterday at Lord's than he began to run for his bowling boots, only to stop in his tracks as the pavilion door framed the figure of Nathan Lyon, last seen so incapacitated as almost to need his own iron lung.

Injured batters have emerged to bat before. Few can have actually hopped down the stairs like a particularly gouty laird. But, having scratched a guard with a tentative left foot, Lyon successfully defended his first few balls by means of a horizontal flap.

When Starc himself proceeded to wear a bouncer in the helmet and underwent a concussion test, Lyon was surrounded by a solicitous cordon of Ben Stokes, Stuart Broad, James Anderson, Ben Duckett, and Josh Tongue, who more doctrinaire commentators would have had telling him to get ready for a broken fucking leg.

For half an hour, each ball was an absurdist cameo. Starc top-edged beyond the boundary, only for a brilliant airborne retrieval by substitute Rehan Ahmed, and a throw by Zak Crawley that nearly caught Lyon short as he limped from one end to other: perhaps the most involuted single in history.

Starc hit a ball to Stokes, who was visibly stricken with cramp;

Starc top-edged a slower ball bouncer and started walking off, only to see the ball just clear Tongue; Starc clonked a six, then was beaten by a wide yorker to expose Lyon to Broad. Or was it to expose Broad to Lyon? For the latter contrived somehow to pull a short ball for four before top-edging to Stokes.

What was this about? England were unlikely to need the time. Australia hardly needed the runs. It was too painful to be a joke; perhaps it was a kind of *ruse de guerre*, the tourists feigning a wounded limp before breaking into a confident stride, like Keyser Soze at the end of *The Usual Suspects*. For with Lyon barely halfway off, Starc vanished up the stairs, and when next seen was bowling very fast indeed.

Lord's has hosted a Test match full of eccentricities. A photograph has been circulated from day three showing Sir Geoffrey Boycott, in the company of his old captain Mike Brearley, apparently shielding his eyes from the atrocious sights—although maybe Brearley had just started talking Wittgenstein again, and Boycott was simply stifling a yawn.

Whatever the case, he can look again. In the battle between ancient tradition and the vagaries of the new age yesterday, orthodoxy and classicism came out well ahead. Defending 371, Australia took four wickets with world-class new-ball bowling strafing the top of off, having watched England toil with methods that must have been based on a mountain of data.

Starc got the ball to swing sharply down the slope, first to snag Crawley's inside edge and then to detonate Pope's middle stump. Cummins unseated Root with a short ball, and then bowled Brook as he looked for a short ball. Good deliveries take wickets. Who knew?

England? Earlier in the day, in the absence of horizontal deviation, Stokes had gone all out for vertical movement, banging the ball in, at lesser velocities than the Australians on Friday, but with a deeper commitment to denial, and fields to match.

Nowhere in the MCC coaching manual or *The Jubilee Book of Cricket* will you encounter a fielding diagram of no slips, one gully, extra cover, fine third man, and a loose daisy chain of four on the on side reinforced by forward square leg on the fence. It looked more like what you might find on Google Maps if you typed in 'pharmacies near me'.

The policy was of necessity as much as choice, compelled by the benignity of the surface, England's lack of express pace and speciality spin, plus the hint of inconsistent bounce when the ball was held cross-seam. And, to be fair, it worked, after a fashion, albeit slowly. Usman Khawaja and Steve Smith, hitherto little troubled, were caught hooking against the slope, Green pulling overconfidently with it. In between times, Root at short leg benefited from Head's pogo stick footwork and Carey's self-protecting glove.

There was also some significantly weird cricket. An easy catch was dropped by Anderson; a new ball was scorned by Stokes. The succession of bouncers induced a kind of trance in the spectators, and also the umpires, from which they were stirred to call only a handful of wides, even when the ball was comfortably clearing the head of the 200cm Green.

To share the burden, Stokes spent much of the lunch break bowling on the outfield trying to loosen his knee, which must be as tenuous now as the string in Captain Mandrake's leg. But he got through a dozen brave overs, badged Green, discomfited Cummins, and took one legitimate wicket and a second with one of five delinquent no balls. Then came the light-hearted Lyon interlude. How we laughed. Until we didn't.

Stumps: England 2nd innings 114/4 (Ben Duckett 50*, Ben Stokes 29*, 31 ov)

2 JULY

Day 5

Let's get this out of the way first. Cricket has some vague statutes. Law 20.1.2 is not one of them. Indeed, it could hardly be more explicit: 'The ball shall be considered to be dead when it is clear to the bowler's end umpire that the fielding side and both batters at the wicket have ceased to regard it as in play.'

So dead ball reflects a view unanimous among players that conveys itself to the umpire. And, errr, that's it. Jonny Bairstow's view yesterday that he was temporarily invulnerable to dismissal was clearly not shared, by his opponents, or the umpires. No, he was not taking a run. That is why he was stumped. I'm glad we had this little chat.

Bairstow wandered off the ground as though unable to credit that the world, so abundant in glad Bazball vibes, could contain such traps and snares. But if his dismissal cost England this Second Test, then what's to blame was his naïveté rather than Alex Carey's alertness.

It didn't anyway. Because the stumping of Bairstow should no more overshadow an epic day's cricket than Nathan Lyon's fumble or Joel Wilson's decision should sour or taint the last afternoon at Headingley in 2019.

This was the Test match day in excelsis: lots of runs to

chase, lots of time to chase them, the spaciousness of five-day cricket seen to the best possible advantage. Nobody explored its bounteous possibilities more splendidly than Ben Stokes, a cricketer it feels an honour to write about.

The scenario before him was different to Headingley 2019, and perhaps even more complex. Four years ago, Stokes had no choice but to hazard everything; here, with more runs to get and more wickets available, he had to temper his approach. Stokes did not always get this balance right: there was one comic moment during their partnership where Stuart Broad guided to deep backward point and made it almost all the way to the opposite end, only to have to backtrack because his captain had not budged.

But when Stokes summed up the St John's Wood Road side of the ground, to which he struck all nine of his sixes, whether the boundary was short, long, medium or otherwise was irrelevant: no ground in the world would have been big enough to contain him. Father Time has seen it all, but would have been pardoned dropping his bail and laying down his scythe to watch.

The day had begun in a low key: no gimmicks, no gimmes, proper batting, committed bowling. Having fought his way back into the game, Mitchell Starc was fast and full, threatening the stumps, the pads and the boots — only an inside edge saved Stokes from the consequences of a yorker.

Ben Duckett, whose laconic manner is a pleasing contrast to the quirks and quiddities of Rory Burns, further enhanced his reputation. He seems to pocket his runs. His most distinctive shot is a minimalist paddle hook, like someone brushing lint off their pants or sweeping dust into a corner.

When Hazlewood succeeded Starc, without a slip and four men on the fence, Duckett still pulled for four, and allowed the next one, slightly shorter, free passage as a wide. The bowler walked back, elbows out, with that slightly stroppy air of his: after an hour, the Australians were starting to sweat. They were relieved when Hazlewood got his length and height right a few overs later, and Duckett edged a hook behind.

While Bairstow was in, Stokes continued abjuring shots he could not keep on the ground; with Bairstow's departure, he kicked out the last of the jams. Broad was brave, stalwart, shrewd. Cummins was, for a time, perplexed, as reflected in his concertina fields, coming in for Broad and out for Stokes—they were a little too reminiscent of the allowances he offered Ajinkya Rahane during the World Test Championship final in order to get at Shardul Thakur.

The Australians, however, showed the benefit of their experience at Headingley in 2019. Their policy of playing slower and aiming wider did, just, prevent Stokes capering away with the game, and eventually persuaded him to depart his plan: hitting towards the Grand Stand, he top-edged Hazlewood. The culpable shot Ollie Robinson then played deserved greater execration than Carey.

Because let's be frank: it was not a day since every other English supporter had found themselves arguing for the letter of the law in the instance of Starc's catch-that-wasn't. Rightly so. This is a Test match. Laws apply with greater force in a skirmish between nations about a border and a dispute between neighbours over a fence.

The booing, as is most booing, was mainly harmless, carrying on as it did long past the point anyone could remember what they were booing, and becoming chiefly about companionship. The parrot cry of 'same old Aussies, always cheating' also invites the question of from whom they might have learned it. After all, you can trace the line of Ashes tit-for-tat back to The Oval in 1882 when, coincidentally, WG Grace ran out the Australian Sammy

Jones for wandering out of his crease under a misapprehension the ball was dead. 'I taught the lad a lesson,' Grace is reputed to have said afterwards; just so.

But the jostling of players in the members'? Really? By virtue of the antiquity of the Long Room, and the assumption that people-like-us know how to behave, Lord's retains the privilege of unusual proximity to the players — the frisson from hearing a players' spikes on the hardwood floor is one of cricket's glories.

They will not have it long, however, if blimps and prigs want to vent fury on their visitors because they are unaware of the laws that … checks notes … their own club sets for the world. And what could be a worse look in the week of the Equity in Cricket report than puce-faced, dimwit snobs picking fights with a placid, softly spoken Muslim player? Chaps, pull yourselves together. You're actually cheating Stokes of some of his glory.

SCOREBOARD

Second Test: Lord's, 28 June–2 July 2023   **Toss:** England
Australia 416 & 279   **England** 325 & 327

Australia won by 43 runs

AUSTRALIA 1ST INNINGS

BATTING		R	B	M	4S	6S	SR
David Warner	b Tongue	66	88	14	8	1	75.00
Usman Khawaja	b Tongue	17	70	107	2	0	24.28
Marnus Labuschagne	c †Bairstow b Robinson	47	93	157	7	0	50.53
Steven Smith	c Duckett b Tongue	110	184	317	15	0	59.78
Travis Head	st †Bairstow b Root	77	73	96	14	0	105.47
Cameron Green	c Anderson b Root	0	3	3	0	0	0.00
Alex Carey †	lbw b Broad	22	43	45	2	0	51.16
Mitchell Starc	c †Bairstow b Anderson	6	10	14	1	0	60.00
Pat Cummins (c)	not out	22	33	64	2	0	66.66
Nathan Lyon	c Tongue b Robinson	7	13	17	1	0	53.84
Josh Hazlewood	c Root b Robinson	4	6	12	1	0	66.66
Extras	(b 13, lb 13, nb 12)	38					
TOTAL	100.4 Ov (RR: 4.13)	416					

Fall of wickets: 1-73 (Usman Khawaja, 23.1 ov), 2-96 (David Warner, 29.5 ov), 3-198 (Marnus Labuschagne, 54.2 ov), 4-316 (Travis Head, 74.2 ov), 5-316(Cameron Green, 74.5 ov), 6-351 (Alex Carey, 84.5 ov), 7-358 (Mitchell Starc, 87.3 ov), 8-393 (Steven Smith, 95.2 ov), 9-408 (Nathan Lyon, 98.4 ov), 10-416(Josh Hazlewood, 100.4 ov)

BOWLING	O	M	R	W	ECON	WD	NB
James Anderson	20	5	53	1	2.65	0	1
Stuart Broad	23	4	99	1	4.30	0	1
Ollie Robinson	24.4	3	100	3	4.05	0	6
Josh Tongue	22	3	98	3	4.45	0	1
Ben Stokes	3	1	21	0	7.00	0	3
Joe Root	8	1	19	2	2.37	0	0

ENGLAND 1ST INNINGS

BATTING		R	B	M	4S	6S	SR
Zak Crawley	st †Carey b Lyon	48	48	81	5	0	100.00
Ben Duckett	c Warner b Hazlewood	98	134	199	9	0	73.13
Ollie Pope	c Smith b Green	42	63	93	4	0	66.66
Joe Root	c Smith b Starc	10	19	39	0	0	52.63
Harry Brook	c Cummins b Starc	50	68	116	4	0	73.52
Ben Stokes (c)	c Green b Starc	17	58	63	1	0	29.31
Jonny Bairstow †	c Cummins b Hazlewood	16	36	58	2	0	44.44
Stuart Broad	lbw b Head	12	24	42	1	0	50.00
Ollie Robinson	c †Carey b Head	9	10	14	1	0	90.00
Josh Tongue	c sub (MT Renshaw) b Cummins	1	4	6	0	0	25.00
James Anderson	not out	0	1	2	0	0	0.00
Extras	(b 9, lb 4, nb 7, w 2)	22					
TOTAL	76.2 Ov (RR: 4.25)	325					

Fall of wickets: 1-91 (Zak Crawley, 17.5 ov), 2-188 (Ollie Pope, 38.1 ov), 3-208 (Ben Duckett, 42.2 ov), 4-222 (Joe Root, 45.3 ov), 5-279 (Ben Stokes, 61.2 ov), 6-293 (Harry Brook, 67.4 ov), 7-311 (Jonny Bairstow, 72.2 ov), 8-324 (Ollie Robinson, 75.1 ov), 9-325 (Stuart Broad, 75.5 ov), 10-325 (Josh Tongue, 76.2 ov)

BOWLING	O	M	R	W	ECON	WD	NB
Mitchell Starc	17	0	88	3	5.17	1	1
Pat Cummins	16.2	2	46	1	2.81	1	0
Josh Hazlewood	13	1	71	2	5.46	0	0
Nathan Lyon	13	1	35	1	2.69	0	0
Cameron Green	9	0	54	1	6.00	0	6
Travis Head	7	1	17	2	2.42	0	0
Steven Smith	1	0	1	0	1.00	0	0

AUSTRALIA 2ND INNINGS

BATTING		R	B	M	4S	6S	SR
Usman Khawaja	c sub (MJ Potts) b Broad	77	187	287	12	0	41.17
David Warner	lbw b Tongue	25	76	107	2	0	32.89
Marnus Labuschagne	c Brook b Anderson	30	51	80	5	0	58.82
Steven Smith	c Crawley b Tongue	34	62	106	5	0	54.83
Travis Head	c Root b Broad	7	16	29	1	0	43.75
Cameron Green	c Duckett b Robinson	18	67	116	3	0	26.86
Alex Carey †	c Root b Robinson	21	73	103	3	0	28.76
Mitchell Starc	not out	15	40	72	1	1	37.50
Pat Cummins (c)	c Duckett b Broad	11	29	32	2	0	37.93
Josh Hazlewood	c Root b Stokes	1	3	9	0	0	33.33
Nathan Lyon	c Stokes b Broad	4	13	25	1	0	30.76
Extras	(b 14, lb 9, nb 6, w 7)	36					
TOTAL	101.5 Ov (RR: 2.73)	279					

Fall of wickets: 1-63 (David Warner, 24.1 ov), 2-123 (Marnus Labuschagne, 40.1 ov), 3-187 (Usman Khawaja, 61.6 ov), 4-190 (Steven Smith, 62.4 ov), 5-197 (Travis Head, 67.3 ov), 6-239 (Cameron Green, 87.3 ov), 7-242 (Alex Carey, 89.1 ov), 8-261 (Pat Cummins, 95.2 ov), 9-264 (Josh Hazlewood, 96.4 ov), 10-279 (Nathan Lyon, 101.5 ov)

BOWLING	O	M	R	W	ECON	WD	NB
James Anderson	19	4	64	1	3.36	0	0
Stuart Broad	24.5	8	65	4	2.61	0	1
Josh Tongue	20	4	53	2	2.65	3	0
Ollie Robinson	26	11	48	2	1.84	2	0
Ben Stokes	12	1	26	1	2.16	1	5

ENGLAND 2ND INNINGS (T: 371 RUNS)

BATTING		R	B	M	4S	6S	SR
Zak Crawley	c †Carey b Starc	3	6	12	0	0	50.00
Ben Duckett	c †Carey b Hazlewood	83	112	224	9	0	74.10
Ollie Pope	b Starc	3	10	13	0	0	30.00
Joe Root	c Warner b Cummins	18	35	40	2	0	51.42
Harry Brook	b Cummins	4	3	4	1	0	133.33
Ben Stokes (c)	c †Carey b Hazlewood	155	214	300	9	9	72.42
Jonny Bairstow †	st †Carey b Green	10	22	32	2	0	45.45
Stuart Broad	c Green b Hazlewood	11	36	125	2	0	30.55
Ollie Robinson	c Smith b Cummins	1	6	6	0	0	16.66
Josh Tongue	b Starc	19	26	49	1	0	73.07
James Anderson	not out	3	23	42	0	0	13.04
Extras	(lb 3, nb 4, w 10)	17					
TOTAL	81.3 Ov (RR: 4.01)	327					

Fall of wickets: 1-9 (Zak Crawley, 2.1 ov), 2-13 (Ollie Pope, 4.2 ov), 3-41 (Joe Root, 12.2 ov), 4-45 (Harry Brook, 12.5 ov), 5-177 (Ben Duckett, 45.4 ov), 6-193(Jonny Bairstow, 51.6 ov), 7-301 (Ben Stokes, 72.1 ov), 8-302 (Ollie Robinson, 73.1 ov), 9-302 (Stuart Broad, 74.2 ov), 10-327 (Josh Tongue, 81.3 ov)

BOWLING	O	M	R	W	ECON	WD	NB
Mitchell Starc	21.3	2	79	3	3.67	3	0
Pat Cummins	25	2	69	3	2.76	2	1
Josh Hazlewood	18	0	80	3	4.44	2	2
Travis Head	4	0	23	0	5.75	0	0
Cameron Green	13	3	73	1	5.61	3	1

3 JULY
CAREY/BAIRSTOW

The mourning after

June in the UK was the hottest on record. How do I know this? Because as yesterday began, I found myself on radio talking about the Lord's Test, Law 20.1.2, Australian perfidy and English virtue, ahead of a later scheduled discussion about climate change.

Except that the talkback lines kept jangling—with a terrific plurality of well-argued and strongly felt opinion, I might add—so that one might have imagined environmental Armageddon to be of strictly secondary importance.

The chatter of talkback and the charivari of social media measure only our most momentary fads and discontents, of course. But, you know what, it felt great. It might have been greater had we been exalting Ben Stokes' homeric 155. Yet it's all of a piece, isn't it? We've been captivated for the last week by brilliant deeds, and now by complex, resonant arguments: no sport, I think, does it better.

For cricket has very particular emotional valencies. When we argue over it, it's often as a proxy for other concerns: our feelings of connection, our anxieties about competition, our fears for the young, and, often as not, where we draw the lines in ethical conduct. This, I might say, distinguishes it from football, perhaps because that sport has grown so bloated as to stand only for itself, and the arc of everything is towards money.

Pardon my Australian's ignorance, and perhaps also my cricketer's uptightness, but I am unable to warm to a game that winks knowingly at diving for penalties — an agreed and protected space for dishonesty.

Not that anyone calls it dishonesty; it hides instead behind the polite euphemism of 'simulation'. Efforts to stamp it out, furthermore, consistently fail, for a good reason given recently by my colleague Matthew Syed: 'Fans do not hate simulation; they love it.' Obviously, there are complex and important reasons why this is so, but don't tell me, because I'm not interested in them.

Which brings us back to Alex Carey's stumping of Jonny Bairstow on Sunday. Because, whatever you may think about it, no dishonesty was involved: it was an open and frank attempt to get the better of a respected opponent.

Carey did not try to deceive Bairstow, or injure him, or intimidate him, or insult him. He did not hide the ball; he did not try to distract Bairstow; he did not push him out of the crease. Carey simply took the ball, rolled it towards the stumps, and caught Bairstow in the act of sleepily wandering forward — just as Bairstow had attempted, unsuccessfully, to catch Labuschagne napping at Edgbaston.

This last fact, furthermore, invalidates the argument that Carey was somehow unsporting because he did not defeat Bairstow with skill. On the contrary, Carey's stumping was full of dexterity: it involved observation, anticipation, skill reproduction under pressure, and originality.

The unusual is sometimes mistaken for the unethical. When BJT Bosanquet invented the googly, some obscurantists decried the notion of pretending to spin the ball one way but actually spinning it the other. Bosanquet himself joked that the googly was 'not illegal, merely immoral'.

The on-field umpires at Lord's did not help things by referring to their off-field colleague what was actually an entirely straightforward decision once the appeal had been issued, given that Bairstow had made no attempt to return to his ground when the stumps were broken.

Had they, alternatively, decided that the ball was dead—a course which was open to them and which they did not take, presumably because they believed it was live—I suspect you'd have had no argument from the Australians. Here was another instance of the stealthy bureaucratisation of officiation that is so simplifying its replacement by technology. Anyway, the very intensity and passion of the exchanges are their own tribute to the Ashes. Had England or Australia been playing any other country, I sincerely doubt that any such discussion would have occurred; it is all the more delicious and provoking for playing to stereotypes of our respective peoples. Had the incident occurred at any ground other than Lord's, the actual font of the game's Laws, the moment would also not have been so inflamed.

This leads us to the utterance of some unpleasantries, in light of the utterly disgraceful conduct on display in the members' stand at lunch on the final day, of which ample, disturbing footage is in circulation, with chants of 'Cheat, cheat, cheat' following the Australians all the way through the Long Room and up the stairs.

The Marylebone Cricket Club is a great institution. Last week, I was there for the quite brilliant launch of an exhibition on the Jewish contribution to cricket: where else in the world, I wondered admiringly, could you find any such thing?

I have immersed myself in the inspirational work of the MCC

Foundation, and been introduced, for instance, to the Alsama Project supporting bottom-of-the-pyramid Syrian refugee children in Lebanon, which uses cricket as part of its educational and rehabilitative initiatives. Would that other private clubs harboured such noble philanthropic instincts.

But seriously? The behaviour of the members towards the Australians, with its public school puerility and reek of entitlement, suggests that the buck needs to stop with Marylebone, rather than start with it. Instead of Lord's being afforded the freedom to police itself, a licence it is hard to imagine being extended to any other venue, the England Cricket Board should be demanding that Marylebone take steps to ensure against a repeat, on pain of the ground's suspension from the Test circuit.

This is all the sharper for the club's status as the arbiter of the game's laws. How can it set an example to the rest of the cricket world when its members behave with such impunity and hypocrisy?

What about the 'spirit of cricket', I hear you, and Rishi Sunak, cry. Granted, there is scope for disagreement about this. But I'd counsel those invoking it to consult the preamble to the Laws — promulgated, of course, by Marylebone. It recommends cricket that is 'hard but fair', advises 'self-discipline, even when things go against you', and demands 'respect for the umpire's decision'. In this, at Lord's, the Australians set an excellent example.

And now ... well, it sure is hot out there, eh?

The road from Sandpapergate to Lord's

Satisfying a controversy as it has been on so many levels, the imbroglio surrounding the stumping of Jonny Bairstow has lacked one thing: a suitably punchy name.

Readers are invited to offer suggestions in the comments. Son of Underarm and/or Jonnyline do not quite suffice, as no contemporary cricket scandal worth the candle is complete without the suffix -gate — affording, of course, a satisfying symmetry with Sandpapergate.

Still, Sandpapergate has, inevitably, come up quite a lot, many treating it as the go-to argument clincher. Australians? Anyone for sandpaper? Haw, haw, haw! Collapse of stout party, etc.

Even m'learned friend Matthew Syed has referred to 'the weight of history that surrounds this team', with the trembling solemnity one might reserve for a crime of imperialism. Yet, in doing so, Syed reveals a dispiritingly narrow perspective of the episode: he elides some facts, omits others, and otherwise plays to that gallery who think it hugely profound to say that sport is about … wait for it … more than winning. Well, d'uh.

When the history of the last decade of Australian cricket comes to be written, Sandpapergate will be one of two episodes to stand out. The other, which helps to understand both this team and its relationship to the Australian public, is the death of Phillip Hughes in November 2014.

We are reminded of this less often, because, frankly, it takes Australians places we would rather avoid: even I, who barely knew Hughes, feeling slightly emotional writing this, remember it as comfortably the worst week of my sportswriting life.

Ironically, Brendon McCullum has spoken, movingly, of the event's impact on his own thinking. Australians have been less obviously candid. It merely peeps through every now and again: Nathan Lyon referred glancingly to the tragedy after the Lord's Test in response to the suggestion, bizarre and offensive, that he batted in the second innings in order to solicit a concussion substitution. And even after all this time, I noticed, he still could not use Hughes' name.

In the wake of Hughes' death, there was a massive spontaneous outpouring of public love for cricket in Australia, if not, at least wholly, for its cricket team. Under the direction at the time of Michael Clarke and Darren Lehmann, and with the encouragement of its administrative classes, Australia had grown into a self-consciously aggressive and abrasive team, convinced that part of their aura was being unpleasant to play against.

There were diverse ways to respond to the trauma of 2014. McCullum has said he went one way: he reassessed his on-field deportment. Australia appeared, to me at least, to trend the opposite way: to try to guts it out, to carry on as before, out of a combination of stoicism and desperation.

Which is also what Cricket Australia (CA) demanded they

do. At the time, we did not question their requirement—it even felt necessary—that the Australian team play a Test match less than a week after Hughes' funeral. They played a full suite of Tests against India—because, of course, we must always play India, because money, because politics, etc.

They powered through a World Cup on adrenalin and testosterone, and then, frankly, it all petered out, in England eight years ago, precipitating the retirements of Clarke, Shane Watson, Brad Haddin, Ryan Harris, Chris Rogers, and Mitchell Johnson within six months.

Age had caught up with them somewhat; but just as much a part of their decisions, I suspect, was a difficulty in feeling quite the same way about cricket. The departures also had the effect of promoting to the captaincy and vice-captaincy Steve Smith and David Warner, superb cricketers, but a coalition with Lehmann that adhered rather than cohered.

Some efforts were made to assist the team through this traumatised time, but I suspect they focused less on actual player welfare than on ensuring that the show went on and the beast was fed.

It was telling that in 2017 the Australian Cricketers' Association fought an ugly pay dispute with CA that was less about money than the players' sense of partnership with their administration, underlain by a worsening sense of mutual distrust. Warner, in particular, took a shop steward's stance, to the extent that some in CA wished his ouster as vice-captain.

So to Sandpapergate, which, there is no avoiding, was a crassly stupid act, if so crassly stupid as to make you wonder quite what madness took hold: it would make a fascinating study in group dynamics. South Africa 2018 was an ugly tour with escalating incidents of player indiscipline on both sides, and some of the most egregious crowd misbehaviour in memory. CA were almost entirely ineffectual: some directors, I suspect, still had their noses out of joint about the pay dispute, and didn't mind Warner, and his wife, getting a bucket of cold sick poured over them every day.

To Sandpapergate there were two waves of response. In Australia, lovers of the game were as unanimously furious as they had been unanimously moved by Hughes' death. Around the rest of the world, meanwhile, spread a sense of schadenfreude, at the bullies ensnared by their own connivances. The Australians had never been popular champions; they had convinced themselves this did not matter; they received a salutary reminder that it did.

Syed is convinced that Lord's demonstrates the Australians' impenitence about Sandpapergate. He furnishes as evidence: 'The Australian cricket board sought to "draw a line" under the affair by conducting an independent inquiry, but—as most people now realise—it was a sham. Only 24 per cent of the Australian players engaged with the process, most refusing to answer the questions of the supposedly thorough inquiry.'

This is erroneous. There were two official responses. One was the inquisition by a CA official, Iain Roy, sent to Cape Town. This certainly could and arguably should have been more thorough, although there was at the time pressure to take action immediately, and the outcome was probably the heaviest sanctions ever imposed on Australian cricketers. The suspensions of Smith, Warner, and Cameron Bancroft, in addition to their desertion by sponsors and their Indian Premier League franchises, cost them millions of dollars.

Syed has conflated this inquiry with CA's subsequent full-scale independent cultural review, led by Sydney's Ethics Centre, whose findings about the organisation's soulless commercialism and abject external relations were so damning that they caused the departure of the chairman and multiple executives.

The players were only one element of this review, and there was no need for them to respond directly to it, because a thorough submission was made on their behalf by the Australian Cricketers' Association.

What about Justin Langer? He was put in to mend the culture, and then the players forced him out, yes? That's only a bit right. Langer's reputation and rigour proved invaluable in the years following Sandpapergate, externally as well as internally: credible, likeable, and a fundamentally good man, he was an excellent public face for the team.

But on the eve of the last Ashes, there was a further scandal that underlined how badly haunted CA remains by Sandpapergate — the defenestration of Tim Paine over an indiscretion for which the organisation had privately cleared him in 2017, but about which they panicked when it threatened to go public, and tried to head off an anticipated fan backlash.

In fact, the public response proved far from monolithic. Some were uneasy about an ancient folly being judged by the new prudery of the age; others, by the obvious double jeopardy of trying Paine twice for the same offence. But the most important medium-term impact was the installation as Paine's successor of Pat Cummins, whose experienced side, after four years with Langer, felt in need of a different coaching touch. CA, who can make the England Cricket Board look like a smooth-running machine, bollocksed this transition up, too.

So the line to be drawn from Sandpapergate to SameOldAussieGate is at best a zig-zag, and exists mainly in the mind of those dwelling in the lowlands of atavistic hatred or the lofty heights of condescension. Paine's successor as gloveman, Alex Carey, furthermore, is a hugely ironic focus of ire, being an exceptionally courteous young man: at Lord's, he did no more than take quicksilver advantage of an opponent's ineptitude, only to find himself paying for animosities lingering from previous generations.

Equally ironic is it to recall that on the eve of the Lord's Test, there were salty old English cricketers deploring that these Ashes were being played in too friendly a spirit. We're never satisfied, are we? I'm surprised it wasn't called Politenessgate.

5 JULY

TOURING LIFE

What happens on tour ...

Touring is not what it was for cricketers, which means it is no longer what it was for the rest of us, whose business it has been to follow them.

An Ashes visit remains the longest undertaken by Australian teams, but is now as short as it has ever been and possibly can be while the playing duration remains five Tests. With the addition of the World Test Championship final, Pat Cummins' team is scheduled more playing than non-playing days: thirty to twenty-four.

This process, of course, has been occurring for as long as I can remember, and the parable of the boiling frog comes to mind, except that in this scenario the frog is amply paid for its boiling. But when you live it, the feeling is different. Essentially, Australia's six Tests are being played in three brackets: twin games separated by three-day gaps for travel and training. This works as a media spectacle: minimal room between matches discourages fans from tuning out and switching off. Yet there is also a greater sense of sanitisation and regimentation. The longer pauses feel like grudging administrative allowances, as though Cricket Australia and the England Cricket Board can't wait until unreliable human materiel is replaced by more congenial and harder-working AI.

The paradox of such tours is that while they are nominally shorter, they are actually more relentless for their lack of breathing space and more tedious for their uniformity. We are in another country, but really in the corporate capsule of CricketWorld, with its ritualistic net sessions, daily player press conferences, and social media watching, from which is derived an almost constant cycle of content. On this tour, I am not only writing for *The Australian* and *The Times*, and dropping in on radio and television, but podcasting: *Cricket Et Cetera*, co-hosted by my colleague of twelve years, Peter Lalor, goes out more or less daily.

Cricket Et Cetera is hardly a professional affair. Neither Pete nor I are technophiles, nor can we take cricket with total seriousness. 'This machine kills fascists,' we say of our podcast recorder, in the spirit of Woody Guthrie and his guitar. It also accommodates a good deal of unstructured chitchat about music, a shared pleasure, and reading, a favoured pastime, plus the odd detour—Soane's Museum and Crossness Pumping Station inter alia.

Perhaps it's the sensation of being managed every day that accounts for our resolute incompetence, our utter refusal to prepare anything in advance, or to do anything that does not first of all please us. Pete likes quoting 'Prisoners of Rock'n'Roll', where Neil Young deplores the record business's homogenising influence: 'That's why we don't want to be good.' So I'm not sure we ever will be.

Occasionally, very occasionally, there is also a chance to play, for which I packed my bat and my box—two things one is loath to share. Yesterday, in fact, I represented the Authors XI as we were hosted by Burghley Park CC on the ancestral estate of Lord Burghley in Lincolnshire, where there are references to cricket as far back as 1771, and where WG Grace is known to have played twice. Overlooked by a picturesque pavilion, the ground slants markedly, and features a ridge as deep as a sand trap. You could have been stepping into a novel by AG Macdonnell.

I've tried to play somewhere on every tour I've made of England—I'm looking forward later on this trip to a game at Arundel. This is not only because I like playing, but because cricket forces you to stop, to wait, to take in your surrounds, to participate in something bigger and longer than the immediate. Yesterday I faced two good quick bowlers, a spinner in his fifties who had only been bowling leg-breaks for nine weeks and was loving it, and a thrower-up of lobs in his sixties who may have been harder to face than anyone because of the possibilities of mortification.

The game was played in jubilant spirit and amid percolating cricket conversation, not least about SameOldAussieGate, upon which there was unanimous agreement that Bairstow was out. Not that there was no scope for leg pulling, as in a celebratory wicket huddle when the next batter in was slow to appear. What about an appeal for timed out? The blame could be placed on the Aussie …

I sat talking for some time after the game to the club historian, Derek Patience. Derek wasn't a player: instead, he was recruited as groundsman thirty years ago on the day he started work as head of grounds at Stamford School. He talked me through some of the club's trials and tribulations, and also its rejuvenation through a week-long twilight six-a-side tournament unfolding in front of us and a crowd of hundreds; there would be thousands for the final on Friday.

So, yes, it's still just possible to leave CricketWorld and see

England, and to touch the fabric of the real game. Because this is where we feel truly connected, where tradition and modernity mix, where the love of cricket is deep and abiding, which is the whole point of what we do. Anyway, now for Leeds. Back to unreality.

The Third Test: Headingley

6–9 July 2023
England won by three wickets

Bazspeed

Life, proverbially, comes at you fast. It hardly came at Australia's cricketers faster than at Headingley in the Third Test, which jammed four innings into 230 overs on the best pitch of the series. Much of the speed was provided by Mark Wood, at last fully fit, who came into the XI with all-rounder Chris Woakes in favour of James Anderson and Josh Tongue: they also had a date with batting destiny.

The other changes were all forced. It was announced that a shoulder injury sustained in the field at Lord's would cost England Ollie Pope's services for the rest of the series, creating a vacancy for Moeen Ali. Nathan Lyon's replacement by Todd Murphy and Hazlewood's resting for Boland had been expected; Cameron Green's supplanting due to a minor leg injury by Mitchell Marsh, less so. In the event, all the changes were consequential, beginning with Marsh's: he dominated Australia's stop-start innings after Stokes again won the toss under a dense bank of cloud.

That innings came after Wood's first electrifying impact, when the visible influence of his speed was corroborated with the empirical evidence of the radar gun. Khawaja, so languid all summer, was bowled through an airy drive by a 96.5 mph

projectile; Labuschagne and Smith were both unsettled before
falling to Woakes and Broad respectively. Marsh brought a big
stride and a powerful pull to the contest, preying on anything
slightly short; even Wood was deposited into the Western
Terrace. But he lacked support besides Head, who was himself
inhibited by an unremitting short-pitched barrage with as many
as four on the fence to leg. After their partnership of 155 in 168
balls, the last six Australians melted in the backdraft of Wood's
jet for 23 runs in 51 deliveries.

Reshuffled for Pope's absence, England's top order struggled
to do much better in the face of a fiery spell from Cummins,
leaving Stokes with the task of repairing the score line of five for
87 after an hour of the second day. England were in danger of
succumbing to a rare excess of caution when, immediately after
lunch, Wood made his second key insurgency of the game: an
eight-ball frolic, including three sixes and a four, as he was tried
and found waiting by the short ball. Wood explained later that for
weeks in the nets he had faced nothing but bouncers; by the time
Australia made their own adjustment, Stokes was unbound. He
had been luckily reprieved on 10, by an umpire's call on Boland,
and temporarily handicapped from 15, with a sore lower back,
his innings dividing into a painstaking 28 off 71 and a punitive
52 off 37. As ever, Australia had their chances: on 45, he was
dropped from consecutive deliveries from Murphy—at long-off
by Starc, and then by the bowler himself, whom he hit for five
sixes in reducing the deficit to 26. Smith marked his hundredth
Test with five catches.

Still, Australia's position looked a strong one. After Warner
fell cheaply to Broad for the second time in the game, Khawaja
and Labuschagne coolly built their advantage, outlasting Wood,
speedy again, and Robinson, missing with back spasms. The pair
treated Moeen with conspicuous respect until just before drinks,

when Labuschagne miscued a slog sweep and Smith aimed a fretful cuff across the line. Khawaja nicked a low catch behind off Woakes, and the fat was again in the fire.

The third day dawned damp on the field and cloudy in the media, with a classic tabloid put-up about Lord's villain Alex Carey not having paid for a haircut in Leeds — except that it wasn't Alex Carey who'd had said haircut, but deputy keeper Jimmy Pierson, who had paid by bank transfer because the salon was cash-only. Apart from that, 100 per cent accurate! At least *The Sun* hadn't hacked Carey's phone for incriminating evidence of a low taper fade, and it kept everyone amused until 4.45 pm when play resumed with thirty-four overs to be bowled. Rain promptly fell again.

Just when fatalism was setting in, however, the sun emerged, followed by the players, and the Test took a further chaotic turn. Marsh was caught behind, and Carey dragged on trying to leave Woakes. Bairstow hesitated after a ball from Wood looped from Starc's glove, requiring Brook to intervene at short leg, and then caught Cummins off Wood securely. Head took Woakes and Wood on, bolting to another half-century, but Broad was able to remove Murphy, and, after two more sixes, Head also. In 115 balls, Australia had added 106 and lost six wickets — perhaps Australia's Bazballiest session of the series, and leaving England with an awkward victory target of 251. In fact, Crawley and Duckett made light of the initial task, knocking 27 runs off the needful in the remaining twenty-four minutes of the day.

On the final morning, Starc struck early to trap Duckett and bowl the ersatz number three, Mooen, while Crawley nicked off after a succession of handsome drives. But back in his number-five slot after an experimental promotion, Brook batted handsomely, as commanding as a Dexter and as casual as a Sehwag. And England always appeared to have a wicket in reserve, although Root and Stokes perished down the leg side either side of lunch, and Bairstow again dragged on. By drinks in the afternoon, thirty-seven runs separated England from victory, with four wickets remaining.

There was just one further alarm, when Starc broke Brook's partnership of 59 in 73 balls with Woakes, while almost denying himself the wicket by trying to interpose beneath the catch that Cummins was about to take. But Wood made sure of the man-of-the-match award by mowing Cummins into the Football Stand, powering Starc through the covers, and top-edging to third man, where the ball fell beyond the reach of the pursuing Carey. The winning runs, a drive through point by Woakes, were almost soothingly orthodox. Woakes and Wood, it transpired, had been travel buddies during the Test. 'We've car-shared all week,' Wood said afterwards. 'We've got a lucky car [parking] space, we've promised that we'd get runs and wickets. I think we will park in the same place every time we turn up here.' It will doubtless be known as Bazparking.

6 JULY

Day 1

Since traditional seasons have dissolved into the stop-start-stop of cricket modernity, it has become possible for players seemingly to vanish—warming benches, receiving treatments, travelling as supernumeraries in baggy squads. The concomitant of this waiting is readiness. Cricket can come like buses: none for ages, then in non-stop succession.

Viz Mitchell Marsh and Mark Wood, waiting earlier this summer, thrust in without delay yesterday, and wasting no time impressing themselves on a fast-moving first day of this Third Test. After all the apprehension about the Australians' welcome, reflected in the phosphorescent outcrops of additional security, the crowd was proper cricket: noisy, supportive, good-humoured, and better behaved than the Marylebone members.

Since he last played a Test four years ago, Mitchell Marsh has made four first-class appearances. There have been more sightings of Lord Lucan. Oh, he has appeared in various white-ball excrescences. More often, thanks to injury, rest periods, schedule lulls, and lately the primacy of his fellow West Australian Cameron Green, Marsh has maintained a sunken profile: two days ago, Cricket Australia withdrew him from The Hundred, to the bemusement of those unaware he had been set to appear.

Before the start at Edgbaston, Marsh was observed sedulously measuring his run, touching off a press box panic about him playing. What a kidder. Such is Green's gilt-edged status, nobody expected Marsh to feature in the Ashes, except maybe Marsh, who has burned off ample surplus energy in the nets and around the grounds: he is the readiest Aussie for a smile, a selfie, an autograph, a chat.

Marsh looked so ripe in his third Test century yesterday, however, that his might almost have been a form pick rather than an injury substitution. The towering thirty-one-year-old is not one of those batters you turn to for effortless timing and touch. A glance at the shoulders and forearms, and the power source is obvious. At times, his power has seemed rather immobile and unfocused; what stood out yesterday was the crisp precision of his footwork rather than the habitual vehemence of his bat swing.

The pitch's pace and carry coaxed bowlers to fuller lengths, offering opportunities to drive; when they overcorrected, Marsh swivelled into a pull as powerful as any in world cricket. There was no waiting in the 90s either, bridged with consecutive straight sixes from Moeen Ali and a hurried single, although his best shot was an on-drive off Woakes — degree of difficulty high, execution perfect.

So precious is Wood's gift of pace, meanwhile, that England have been loath to spend it frivolously. It's as though he has already been budgeted his lifespan's deliveries, and they are not to be squandered on, for example, the mundanity of county cricket, of which he has played three games in the last five years. But you can see why. Two spells yesterday changed the summer's dynamic — Bazball had previously been Bazbat rather than Bazbowl.

By the first spell, even the easeful Khawaja was hastened; Labuschagne, who has favoured batting forward of his crease against England's seamers this summer, shrank back inside, and stood taller, wrists cocked, as if in an iron maiden of defence. There were oooohs and aaaahs as Wood's speeds were carded, eventually revealing a full house of deliveries in the mid-90s. A couple of times, the ball passed Labuschagne's outside edge and he held his shape as though to dramatise the discrepant nature of the bowler's pace — the game seemed to be happening at two speeds.

For some reason, Wood always puts me in mind of that Georgian prizefighter Hen Pearce — Pearce's flavoursome nickname 'The Game Chicken' would work with Wood's bantam physique and perky character, the way he bounces to his feet after occasionally falling in his follow-through. Now the Game Chicken bowled Khawaja through an airy drive, with a delivery that took such a gash from the ball it needed replacing. Although, did Wood need replacing with figures of 4–3–2–1? In succession, Ollie Robinson's marshmallow bouncers looked even softer than usual. And should Wood have bowled as few as half a dozen of the first 34 overs of Australia's innings?

On returning in the afternoon, Wood could not summon quite the same propulsion: Marsh pulled him for six dismissively, smashed him straight and through the covers, as his partnership with a subdued Travis Head swelled to 158 in 168 balls.

After Marsh's dismissal on the stroke of tea, however, Wood dissolved Australia's tail like battery acid, bowling Starc with a trimmer that swung back to hit top of middle, trapping Cummins with a ball that would have hit middle of middle, and forcing a flail from Carey and a shank from Murphy. How useful that extra turn of speed would have been at Edgbaston.

In fact, England will regard their dismissing Australia for 263 as a good day's work up to the point they recall that they might have dismissed them for 163. Head (on 9) was dropped at the wicket: we're at the point where Bairstow's wicketkeeping is a breach of the spirit of cricket. Marsh (on 12) was dropped at first slip by Root: as of last night, England's series record is fifteen drops and a flubbed stumping, which is probably the fault of those uncouth colonials for hitting the ball too hard.

Australia also just shaded the day when Marsh, in his second over, induced a characteristic poke from Zak Crawley, who had to that stage played regally: not even Marsh hit anything as hard as Crawley's shot on the rise through mid-wicket off Cummins, which bounced back 15 metres from the fence. Bairstow was then beaten by his third delivery and immediately went wandering down the pitch, only to pull himself up and pedantically drop his bat in the crease. Oh, Jonny be good. No boundary was scored in a tense last ten overs, but otherwise there has been no waiting, no delay in this Third Test. With 331 runs in a day for thirteen wickets, it is surging.

Stumps: Australia 1st innings 263. England 1st innings 68/3 (Joe Root 19*, Jonny Bairstow 1*, 19 ov)

7 JULY

Day 2

In the last week, Pat Cummins and Ben Stokes have been seen in the variety of guises that Test captains must sometimes otherwise assume: figureheads, advocates, ambassadors, even philosophers, publicly comparing notes about rightful stances on laws, spirits, and points between.

Irrespective of one's opinion on the matter, both have made good impressions. Cummins has managed not to sound prickly and defensive; Stokes has come off as neither preachy nor pious. Neither has shifted position; both have kept their heads, when all about them have been positively ripping theirs off.

Yet with the flip of the coin at Headingley would surely have come a sense of relief at swapping words, slippery things, for deeds, susceptible to will and skill. Stokes gained the initial advantage and threw out the first challenge, sending Australia in and seeing them bowled out summarily enough that not only his bowlers but his batters have enjoyed considerably the better conditions here. But on this second day, Cummins helped make the game like the last US election wasn't: too close to call.

Great interest attended how England would tackle their chase of the visitors' 263. Some, mainly in Australia, think Bazball already dead; others, mainly in England, think that long may she wave. One suspects that, like Kenny in *South Park*, it will always be being killed off, only to be either updated (New Improved Bazball, Now With Added Golf), or revisited (Bazball Classique, Original Formula).

Before lunch yesterday, however, confusion seemed to reign. England played as though Bazball was a once-familiar tune they could not quite recall, interspersing long periods of passivity with shots of seeming casualness: a compulsive glide from Joe Root in the first over, a listless drive from Jonny Bairstow, wafty hooks from Moeen Ali and Chris Woakes. After lunch, Wood and Broad had a handy thrash. But without Stokes, as at Headingley four years ago, there would have been little worth speaking of.

The toll of the intervening years was there for all to see. In that magical Test match in 2019, Stokes bowled 24 back-breaking overs, before executing perhaps cricket's greatest momentum shift: having eked three singles out of 73 balls, he gouged 132 runs from the next 146. Now Stokes can bowl only in emergencies, and his mighty oaken strength is plagued by burrs and burls. On 10, he should by rights have been lbw to Boland, only to survive an umpire's call. On 45, his miscue fell luckily into open space just short of the approaching Starc. Later, Stokes was visibly discomfited by what was probably a painful right glute, and thrice sank to his knees when Starc hit him on the upper part of the thigh; the last time, he genuflected over his bat like a knight swearing allegiance in Camelot.

Still, who could not be inspired by Stokes' might and main? Between some gloriously expansive shots, he moved round the crease with all the grace of a pirate on his peg. As the innings expired around him, Stokes briefly mauled the Ashes newbie Todd Murphy, taking advantage of the short straight boundaries. Murphy showed willing, however, and Cummins stuck with him, until a vertical mishit provided Smith with his fifth catch in the innings. Another stirring innings from Stokes; another examination passed by Murphy; and a trick won by Cummins.

Otherwise, Cummins chose the day to take his first five-for in England, in his ninth Test here: a strangely belated achievement, but in the context of an attack where the competition for a finitude of wickets is intense. He has tended instead to grab important scalps: critically, Root, who averages only 22.6 against him, ten times. Now he appeared to transfix his targets. Moeen mishooked luckily into space, then immediately played an identical shot straight to the fielder.

In the later stages, one appreciated the predicament of the fast-bowling captain—Cummins standing at the end of his run, sweat pouring off him, trying to work out what to bowl when, even as he decided where everyone should stand then. He shifted and shuffled; he waved and beckoned; then he charged in again to his opposite number, who four years ago had so spectacularly got the better of him. To stop Stokes at 80 would have felt like a victory, however temporary.

Cummins might have the Indian sign on Root, but Broad must have a virtual voodoo doll for Warner, now with seventeen pins. Since Broad started working Warner over from around the wicket, so that his defensive bat closes slightly and his left shoulder comes round, replays have almost needed a déjà vu warning. Australia has ten days to decide his future. Could they possibly leave him out for Old Trafford? It would be like the Huns dropping Attila.

Warner's fate may yet depend on the result here, which by the close was deliriously unclear. Australia's lead was nearly 100 when Labuschagne and Smith caught the bug of feckless shots, becoming wickets 199 and 200 of Moeen's protracted, retracted, detracted career.

The wicket that really mattered was Khawaja's, who maintained his sang froid even during another blood-and-thunder spell from Mark Wood, during which Bairstow stood closer to the boundary than the stumps. Then—sod's law—Khawaja got the finest of nicks to Bairstow off Woakes. As on the first day, Mitchell Marsh and Travis Head formed a protective barrier. But what are the odds that this absorbing Test resolves, as it did in 2019, into a final-day duel between Cummins and Stokes?

Stumps: England 1st innings 237. Australia 2nd innings 116/4 (Travis Head 18*, Mitchell Marsh 17*, 47 ov)

8 JULY

Day 3

Smith and Labuschagne. Labuschagne and Smith. Whichever way you order the crack Australian pair, by seniority or alphabet, they almost deserve a portmanteau nickname à la Bennifer and Hiddleswift. Anyone for SmithoSchagne? Or MarnuSmudge?

It's not just we who elide them; they do themselves. When in proximity, they reputedly do everything together; when apart, these cricket savants reportedly talk every day, at length, and not about the situation in Ukraine or their prize geraniums. They discuss batting, at such a level of granularity that they might as well be speaking in tongues.

They have been discussed in relation to one another ever since that unforgettable interlude four years ago when Labuschagne substituted for a concussed Smith at Lord's, coming to stay. In recent times, the pair have formed the spinal column of Australian batting: second and third on the ICC Test rankings, and the only batters of their generation to explore the far side of a 60 average.

So tightly have they tracked one another, in fact, that there is a certain piquancy about their slight but parallel eclipse in these Ashes. It's relative, of course, rather than abject: after all, Smith was man-of-the-match at Lord's. But their failures at Headingley have given England an excellent chance in a compelling and intriguing Test.

Labuschagne, as has been his recent wont, made two starts, only to nick off in the first innings and hole out in the second, essaying a slog sweep—only the sixth such shot he has played in his Test career, half of which have dismissed him.

Smith's hundredth Test has been a strange affair. In the first innings, having uncharacteristically wellied an early six, he uncharacteristically reviewed a caught-behind verdict when he had clearly hit the ball; second time around, he picked out a short mid-wicket, hitting across a ball tossed into the breeze, and then took unnecessary offence at a very mild quip from Bairstow.

Labuschagne has now made one half-century in his last sixteen starts, which was in the second innings of the Ahmedabad Test on a pitch where they could still be playing. What's been a wrinkle in his career, moreover, has gradually become a fold: his home record (2,397 runs at 70) is more or less twice his away record (1,028 runs at 36). Some observers during this Ashes series have noted him crowding off stump; others have critiqued his over-eagerness to get bat on ball.

Four years ago, meanwhile, nothing short of a blow on the conk could stop the mighty Smith. His Test average peaked at 65, built on twenty-six hundreds. Since then, with bowlers testing him out on shorter lengths and leg-side lines, he has reverted a little to the mean, averaging 46, with half-a-dozen hundreds more. Still formidable, but closer to mortal.

At the top of summer, Smith reintroduced to his set-up the back-and-across step he had briefly discarded. But especially at Edgbaston, England troubled him by coming wide of the crease, and two indeterminate innings were the result.

So what is amiss? Is it technique? Is it the familiarity of their methods to observant rivals? Or is it something more akin to a short circuit or a flipped switch? Like a cricket washing machine and/or tumble dryer, Labuschagne and Smith consume an outsize amount of energy. Perhaps in drawing so heavily on the grid, they've burned a fuse or two.

Labuschagne this summer seems to have lacked his signature vitality. Missing have been that mark-of-Zorro leave, that parade ground bark of 'No run!', and those gassy short-leg monologues, for all of which Labuschagne used to be rather mocked, but which coincided with his signal phase of success. The World Test Championship final provided the curious sight of Labuschagne having a siesta as he waited to go into bat. Oh Marnus! How we laughed. But maybe it was a leading indicator.

Smith, of course, never presents as other than a fascinating study on the field, with all his tics and his twitches, his early seeing and late playing. But there may also be something significant about his regimen off the field. During Test matches, Smith is a notoriously terrible sleeper, often playing at the brink of exhaustion. In his recent book *Not Out* (2021), Greg Chappell described coming across Smith in the middle of a big hundred in Perth, sitting on a physiotherapist's table staring sightlessly into space and looking like a 'shell of a man'. When Chappell remarked on this, Smith complained: 'Oh mate, I'm gone. I can't sleep, I'm not eating … During a Test match I can't do anything. All I can do is play cricket and stagger back to my room.'

Now that Smith is thirty-four, there is some empirical evidence that the deeper a match goes, the less Smith is a factor. His averages across the four innings of Test matches are, respectively, 86, 55, 43, and 28 — quite a pronounced tapering, given the sample size of a century of five-day games.

His summer has also fallen into something like that pattern. In the World Test Championship final, after a few months off, Smith batted with sublime control, only to fail in the Edgbaston

Test that followed hard on that match's heels. Smith then looked fresh and free in the Lord's Test, but has failed here after another three-day turnaround. Early English dawns and late dusks are always a challenge for visiting Australians. And as any new parent will tell you, not even a Leeds barber demands repayment so urgently as a sleep debt.

These days we have so much data at our disposal, such comprehensive analytical tools and such brilliant interpreters and expositors among our commentariat, that we incline towards examining the modern batter as a kind of automata. They are doing this; they are not doing that; this is what the coaches will be saying; this is how the batter must adjust. Why rather than how a player loses their way is far harder to answer. But even those as accomplished as Labosteve are mere flesh and blood.

Stumps: Australia 2nd innings 224. England 2nd innings 27/0 (Zak Crawley 9*, Ben Duckett 18*, 5 ov)

9 JULY

Day 4

Now it gets interesting. Or, at least, it gets more interesting, because it's never been other than interesting, with fourteen out of a possible fifteen days played, and now a third squeaker. Whoever loses these Ashes may end up regretting only one or two failures and/or misfortunes; whoever wins can count themselves lucky. They are that close.

Either team by now could be leading 3–0, or trailing 0–3. As it is, should England win at Old Trafford, we would be set at two-all for a Fifth Test decider, which has happened only thrice in the annals of cricket's most storied series.

Let's not get ahead of ourselves. There is nothing inevitable about this in such a supremely evitable series. But, for just an instant, entertain the fantasy. In theory, an uneven number of games sets itself up to be decided by the odd game at the end. In practice, the trend has latterly been towards blow-outs. No longer.

The Ashes of 2023 has already been of exceptionally high quality, and also strewn with mistakes. Yesterday, two Australians almost collided taking a catch like Aussie rules ruckmen competing at a stoppage, and their spinner bowled a huge no ball at a clutch moment. One English batter reviewed an lbw when the ball was going gun-barrel straight, while two fell to leg-side strangles.

This is not a paradox so much as an inevitability. Two teams hurling themselves at each other so hard will generate error much as chips fly off marble being worked. Each team has tripped themselves up, and also fought back brilliantly.

We arrived at Headingley drawing on memories of four years ago, and parallels could be detected. England had by far the better of the conditions; they prevailed in part by retarding Australia's progress in the third innings. But this was a more accomplished, or at least more replicable, success. No miracle innings was needed; no fumble or umpiring favour intervened.

England's order played with purpose in the second innings all the way down—254 in 50 overs is a standard one-day chase—and their match winners were a memorable combination. There was Harry Brook, who had struggled to work his way into these Ashes hitherto, and Chris Woakes, who has struggled to work his way into the Ashes full stop.

In the ten years since Woakes' debut, he has twice previously been part of a successful Ashes team, victories to which he had contributed 14 runs and three wickets. He is a better cricketer than that, as he showed yesterday with a calmly deliberate unbeaten 32 to go with his half-dozen important wickets.

There was a sense that a brief thrust might tilt things. Stokes, ever inventive, hazarded an experiment at number three by promoting Moeen, perhaps to cushion Brook, perhaps to introduce a disruptive left-hander, although Starc bowled him through a defence that gaped like Nigel Farage's mouth.

Root aimed a wide drive at his first ball, and was fortunate enough to miss; Crawley made a wide drive at Starc, which Green might have caught in the gully, but the heavier-set Marsh was a little slower to rise. In general, the fielding was first rate, the sweepers busy, the chases keen, the throws flat, and Labuschagne excelling in front of the wicket on the off side.

At two for 82, a replacement ball started to swing and bounce for Marsh, drew Crawley into an overeager drive, and at last exposed Brook. He had emerged in the gloaming on the first night and looked a beat behind. Boland cut him in half with a delivery that jagged back, but he pilfered three boundaries, and a fourth when Starc offered width. Killer stat: nobody has got to 1,000 Test runs faster in balls faced.

England looked well set up at lunch, but Starc came back up the hill to Stokes, where the bounce was a little less predictable and his effortless knots invaluable, producing what in its way was a classic Starc wicket. I know, I know: a leg-side strangle. But here is Starc's peculiar menace — that with his rapid, unpredictable, left-arm sling, he opens angles accessible to nobody else in world cricket.

Bairstow played his second wretched, soft-headed drive of the match, this time connecting with the inside rather than the outside edge, and the match was back in the balance. But the 59-run, 73-ball partnership of Brook and Woakes was full of judicious stroke play and alert running. Cummins bowling short to the long leg-side boundary with four men back to Woakes, but not pursuing the same gambit against Brook was a peculiar bit of captaincy; Boland at third man not attacking Wood's top edge off Starc, and leaving it to Carey, was a diffident act of fielding.

Did Australia just blink here? Wood does everything fast: you can imagine him trying to set records for drinking a pint or tying his laces. And he was just who no captain would want to see batting at number nine, where he is never knowingly outdared. He had confounded Cummins and limited England's deficit on Friday; now, with six men on the fence, he could have taken a single in every direction. But that is not how he, or England, roll.

Remember: this was only the fourth day of a game spanning just 230 overs that produced only one century and three fifties, yet seemed to last an aeon. It's just a bit incredible; it might get even more so.

SCOREBOARD

Third Test: Leeds, 6–9 July 2023   **Toss:** England
Australia: 263 & 224   **England:** 237 & 254/7

England won by 3 wickets

AUSTRALIA 1ST INNINGS

BATTING		R	B	M	4S	6S	SR
David Warner	c Crawley b Broad	**4**	5	3	1	0	80.00
Usman Khawaja	b Wood	**13**	37	60	2	0	35.13
Marnus Labuschagne	c Root b Woakes	**21**	58	84	4	0	36.20
Steven Smith	c †Bairstow b Broad	**22**	31	52	1	1	70.96
Travis Head	c Root b Woakes	**39**	74	153	5	0	52.70
Mitchell Marsh	c Crawley b Woakes	**118**	118	120	17	4	100.00
Alex Carey †	c Woakes b Wood	**8**	16	32	1	0	50.00
Mitchell Starc	b Wood	**2**	10	7	0	0	20.00
Pat Cummins (c)	lbw b Wood	**0**	2	2	0	0	0.00
Todd Murphy	b Wood	**13**	12	21	3	0	108.33
Scott Boland	not out	**0**	4	10	0	0	0.00
Extras	(b 10, lb 10, nb 3)	**23**					
TOTAL	**60.4 Ov (RR: 4.33)**	**263**					

Fall of wickets: 1-4 (David Warner, 0.5 ov), 2-42 (Usman Khawaja, 12.6 ov), 3-61 (Marnus Labuschagne, 19.3 ov), 4-85 (Steven Smith, 24.2 ov), 5-240 (Mitchell Marsh, 52.1 ov), 6-245 (Travis Head, 54.3 ov), 7-249 (Mitchell Starc, 56.3 ov), 8-249 (Pat Cummins, 56.5 ov), 9-254 (Alex Carey, 58.2 ov), 10-263 (Todd Murphy, 60.4 ov)

BOWLING	O	M	R	W	ECON	WD	NB
Stuart Broad	11.4	0	58	2	4.97	0	1
Ollie Robinson	11.2	2	38	0	3.35	0	2
Mark Wood	11.4	4	34	5	2.91	0	0
Chris Woakes	17	1	73	3	4.29	0	0
Moeen Ali	9	1	40	0	4.44	0	0

ENGLAND 1ST INNINGS

BATTING		R	B	M	4S	6S	SR
Zak Crawley	c Warner b Marsh	33	39	65	3	0	84.61
Ben Duckett	c †Carey b Cummins	2	6	15	0	0	33.33
Harry Brook	c Smith b Cummins	3	11	9	0	0	27.27
Joe Root	c Warner b Cummins	19	45	66	2	0	42.22
Jonny Bairstow †	c Smith b Starc	12	37	51	2	0	32.43
Ben Stokes (c)	c Smith b Murphy	80	108	166	6	5	74.07
Moeen Ali	c Smith b Cummins	21	46	69	2	0	45.65
Chris Woakes	c †Carey b Starc	10	10	16	0	1	100.00
Mark Wood	c Marsh b Cummins	24	8	8	1	3	300.00
Stuart Broad	c Smith b Cummins	7	8	21	1	0	87.50
Ollie Robinson	not out	5	6	22	1	0	83.33
Extras	(b 4, lb 3, nb 9, w 5)	21					
TOTAL	52.3 Ov (RR: 4.51)	237					

Fall of wickets: 1-18 (Ben Duckett, 3.2 ov), 2-22 (Harry Brook, 5.2 ov), 3-65 (Zak Crawley, 13.3 ov), 4-68 (Joe Root, 19.2 ov), 5-87 (Jonny Bairstow, 24.3 ov), 6-131 (Moeen Ali, 39.4 ov), 7-142 (Chris Woakes, 42.1 ov), 8-167 (Mark Wood, 43.4 ov), 9-199 (Stuart Broad, 47.4 ov), 10-237 (Ben Stokes, 52.3 ov)

BOWLING	O	M	R	W	ECON	WD	NB
Mitchell Starc	14	3	59	2	4.21	0	1
Pat Cummins	18	1	91	6	5.05	1	3
Scott Boland	10	0	35	0	3.50	0	3
Mitchell Marsh	3	1	9	1	3.00	0	2
Todd Murphy	7.3	0	36	1	4.80	0	0

AUSTRALIA 2ND INNINGS

BATTING		R	B	M	4S	6S	SR
Usman Khawaja	c †Bairstow b Woakes	43	96	159	3	0	44.79
David Warner	c Crawley b Broad	1	5	13	0	0	20.00
Marnus Labuschagne	c Brook b Ali	33	77	102	5	0	42.85
Steven Smith	c Duckett b Ali	2	9	13	0	0	22.22
Travis Head	c Duckett b Broad	77	112	201	7	3	68.75
Mitchell Marsh	c †Bairstow b Woakes	28	52	65	5	0	53.84
Alex Carey †	b Woakes	5	14	20	1	0	35.71
Mitchell Starc	c Brook b Wood	16	19	25	2	0	84.21
Pat Cummins (c)	c †Bairstow b Wood	1	8	11	0	0	12.50
Todd Murphy	lbw b Broad	11	10	37	2	0	110.00
Scott Boland	not out	0	1	11	0	0	0.00
Extras	(b 5, lb 2)	7					
TOTAL	67.1 Ov (RR: 3.33)	224					

Fall of wickets: 1-11 (David Warner, 2.2 ov), 2-68 (Marnus Labuschagne, 25.2 ov), 3-72 (Steven Smith, 27.4 ov), 4-90 (Usman Khawaja, 34.5 ov), 5-131 (Mitchell Marsh, 49.5 ov), 6-139 (Alex Carey, 53.5 ov), 7-168 (Mitchell Starc, 58.4 ov), 8-170 (Pat Cummins, 60.2 ov), 9-211 (Todd Murphy, 65.5 ov), 10-224 (Travis Head, 67.1 ov)

BOWLING	O	M	R	W	ECON	WD	NB
Stuart Broad	14.1	3	45	3	3.17	0	0
Chris Woakes	18	0	68	3	3.77	0	0
Mark Wood	17	2	66	2	3.88	0	0
Joe Root	1	0	4	0	4.00	0	0
Moeen Ali	17	3	34	2	2.00	0	0

ENGLAND 2ND INNINGS (T: 251 RUNS)

BATTING		R	B	M	4S	6S	SR
Zak Crawley	c †Carey b Marsh	**44**	55	100	5	0	80.00
Ben Duckett	lbw b Starc	**23**	31	46	3	0	74.19
Moeen Ali	b Starc	**5**	15	22	0	0	33.33
Joe Root	c †Carey b Cummins	**21**	33	72	3	0	63.63
Harry Brook	c Cummins b Starc	**75**	93	139	9	0	80.64
Ben Stokes (c)	c †Carey b Starc	**13**	15	25	2	0	86.66
Jonny Bairstow †	b Starc	**5**	8	9	1	0	62.50
Chris Woakes	not out	**32**	47	75	4	0	68.08
Mark Wood	not out	**16**	8	14	1	1	200.00
Extras	(b 7, lb 7, nb 5, w 1)	**20**					
TOTAL	**50 Ov (RR: 5.08)**	**254/7**					

Did not bat: Ollie Robinson, Stuart Broad

Fall of wickets: 1-42 (Ben Duckett, 9.1 ov), 2-60 (Moeen Ali, 13.5 ov), 3-93 (Zak Crawley, 19.3 ov), 4-131 (Joe Root, 28.5 ov), 5-161 (Ben Stokes, 33.5 ov), 6-171(Jonny Bairstow, 35.5 ov), 7-230 (Harry Brook, 47.4 ov)

BOWLING	O	M	R	W	ECON	WD	NB
Pat Cummins	15	0	77	1	5.13	0	1
Mitchell Starc	16	0	78	5	4.87	1	0
Scott Boland	11	1	49	0	4.45	0	2
Mitchell Marsh	6	0	23	1	3.83	0	1
Todd Murphy	2	0	13	0	6.50	0	1

10 JULY
STUART BROAD

The best of frenemies

Ben Stokes is mighty. Mark Wood is fast. Joe Root and Harry Brook are quality. But Australians can't look away from the Englishman who, day in, day out, is doing most to rake over the 2023 Ashes: that familiar antagonist, Stuart Broad.

Broad has just turned 37 — too old, surely, for the affectation of the headband that makes him look like a cosplay samurai. But, y'know, that's Broad all over. At 198 cm, he cannot help but stand out, so goes with it. He throws out provocations — the celebrappeals, the crowd conducting, the voiding of those Ashes series he prefers to forget.

And, gallingly for Australians, he backs them up. Nobody has delivered more overs (117.4) or taken more wickets (16 at 24.9) in these three Tests. He's bowled beautifully, batted bravely, and been as big a nuisance as ever.

That it was Broad who succeeded Bairstow in the wake of the latter's stumping at Lord's, for example, could hardly have been more exquisite. Here's the guy who stood still as a statue when he smashed a caught behind at Trent Bridge ten years ago, handing out etiquette lessons. The audacity of that is just ... magnificent.

I hardly agree with him that it was 'the worst thing I've ever seen in cricket'—for me, that was probably Narendra Modi and Anthony Albanese at Modi Stadium earlier this year. But how I enjoyed his response: the theatricality of him lipping Alex Carey, and checking the crease every over was just so ... Broad.

Then, when it was done, the perfectly drawn line and succinct tweet: 'A great Ashes battle. Loved being out there with @ benstokes38 in that mood. Some controversial moments that will split opinions, that's sport. Lord's as loud & animated as I've ever heard it. On to Leeds we go!'

Too right, and that's Broad also. He goes all-in; he comes straight out. Which, dare I say it, is very Australian: he is an uncompromising competitor unclouded by animosities. We Australians have loved to hate him; for a while now, I suspect we've hated to love him, just a little. He's the guy that Aussies most want to get the better of; he's the guy Aussies would probably most enjoy a beer with, not least for owning his own pub.

Australians can take a modest share of him also. His cricket heroes growing up were the Aussies of the Warne-McGrath-Ponting era: 'They were so successful. They were winners.' And it was an Australian summer in 2004–5 for Hoppers Crossing Cricket Club in the Victorian Turf Cricket Association that Broad, then eighteen, has said was the making of him.

'I went over as a young kid,' Broad has recalled. 'Public school cricket, all nicey-nicey, flat wickets, knock it around ... and then I stepped out there, and it was like being in a fight.'

Broad lived with the groundsman, worked as a brickie and a gardener during the week, played tough cricket at the weekend, and discovered he liked it; he developed what you can only call a Broad streak of Australian pragmatism. Which, of course, was on show that day in Nottingham, for which I've defended him in 1,000 Aussie conversations.

In Charlie Macartney's autobiography, the great Australian batter of 100 years ago described being scolded by no less than Victor Trumper for giving himself out in a game: it's a cardinal principle that Australians neither trespass on the umpire's job nor question the umpire's decision.

Besides, Trent Bridge was an Australian stuff-up. Earlier in the afternoon, they had idly torched the review they later needed. The fairest way to evaluate Ashes disputes, as I see it, is to imagine the alleged misdeed being perpetrated by your opponent. No Australian would have walked in similar circumstances. Why should Broad have? (Likewise, I'd have had no complaint had the roles of Bairstow and Carey at Lord's been reversed.)

Something else to be respected is that Broad keeps coming back for more, has been prepared to fight for his place, has been proud but never entitled. Eighteen months ago, of course, he seemed to have been discarded, as Joe Root struggled with his captaincy's impending doom, and Chris Silverwood did his final impersonation of tight-lipped, ashen-faced supremo Ron Knee.

Broad's column in the *Daily Mail*, never perfunctory, sometime disarmingly frank, described a kind of grief response to his omission: 'Not to big it up too much but it has affected my sleep. I said to my partner Mollie one morning that my body felt sore. She suggested that would be stress. No, I can't pretend I am as good as gold, because I am not. It would be wrong to act like everything's OK.' The public relished James Anderson's redemption song, but it's been Broad who has really held the tune.

Since working his passage back, Broad has taken 61 wickets at 25 — better than his career average. He is now two Test wickets away from 600, and three from 150 in the Ashes. There is a very good chance that David Warner, whom he has dismissed seventeen times, will be one of them.

You could write volumes on this still unfolding rivalry, but one of its more fascinating elements is its playing out against a vaguely opposite overall trend. Broad has played in thirty-eight Ashes Tests, won twelve, and lost eighteen; Warner has played thirty-one, won nineteen, and lost seven.

There is all of cricket in that. Broad has enjoyed the individual edge, while Warner has formed part of a collective edge. We are probably in the last stages of savouring this endlessly fascinating game within the game, this interpersonal Ashes, which, let's not forget, has spanned a decade, not just a couple of series. Bring it on.

14 JULY
DAVID WARNER

Not going gentle

It took thirty seconds for the first SMS to come from Australia. David Warner had just been dismissed in the first innings at Birmingham, and a female friend, far from a hardcore cricket devotee, wanted me to know: 'I just don't understand why David Warner still gets a guernsey.'

Everyone has a view on David Warner. Everyone has always had a view on David Warner. His whole career has occurred amid a din of opinion, not that said opinion has always been entirely about him.

Since he first represented Australia, without so much as the by-your-leave of a first-class cap, Warner has had a sizeable symbolic quotient: your perspective of him is likely also an expression of your ideas about Australia, about modern cricket, about professional sport more generally. He is arguably the first Australian athlete to have his biggest fan base in India, where he has been the most successful foreign batter in the Indian Premier League and the hardest-working cricketer on TikTok.

Right now, everyone will have an opinion on Warner's

entitlement to a place in Australia's XI for next Wednesday's Old Trafford Test, so effectively has he been nullified by Stuart Broad. Last week at Headingley, Warner cuffed the first ball of the Test for four, but in nine further deliveries contrived to nick off to Broad twice, for the sixteenth and seventeenth time in Tests.

With the exception of a mighty double hundred in the Boxing Day Test, furthermore, Warner has found pickings thin for some time. It was not the end when he was invalided out of the Border-Gavaskar Trophy at Delhi, but it was a memento mori: in his last Test innings in India, it emerged, Warner was battling a sore head and a fractured arm, although he was still irked to fail a concussion test on the odd answer.

Whatever might be said of Warner, he has always shown willing. It was widely thought that suspension would be the end of him. He was permanently tainted; he was disbarred from captaincy; low-hanging franchise-cricket fruit must have been sorely tempting.

Nor, in run terms, can his return to the colours be said to have entirely paid off: exclude that bloated triple century against a puny Pakistan attack in December 2019, and his average across the other thirty-two Tests drops to less than 30.

But by declining to slip away in disgrace, by sucking up the odium and humiliation of Sandpapergate, Warner has conveyed something of the sense of honour he derives from playing for Australia. For a cricketer so identified with the new, his is a working-class conservative core. I have never known him to complain of burnout; he has never asked for a tour off, or sought a middle-order bolt hole.

So what has gone amiss in Warner's game? His batting model was always built on the punishment of width. His jubilant meat-cleaver cut was a feature of his first four Ashes series, in all of which Broad played, in which Warner averaged nearly 50.

But even then the dynamics of right-arm pace to left-handed batters was changing: more than half of it these days is delivered from around the wicket, compared to barely a fifth when Warner's career began. As they've had more practice from this angle, quicks have improved at it, too, sacrificing fewer knots and locating top-of-off lengths more consistently.

Left-handed batters have traditionally succeeded in cricket in outsize proportion, relative to left-handedness's incidence in the population. Lately, however, that advantage has been somewhat eroded: Usman Khawaja, Travis Head, Dimuth Karunaratne, and Devon Conway are not the force that Kumar Sangakkara, Matthew Hayden, Justin Langer, Mike Hussey, Adam Gilchrist, Andy Flower, and Graeme Smith were twenty years ago.

In England, furthermore, Broad is formidable. With his new aptitude for taking the ball away from right-handers, he challenges both edges, while the lower bounce brings lbw into play. Warner also now sees so little width that he is inclined to seize on it overenthusiastically, as he did at Edgbaston when, hopelessly off balance, he dragged Broad onto his stumps (and earlier, in the World Test Championship final, when he tried to force Mohammad Siraj off the back foot in the second innings).

So what will Australia do? Since Warner set his own Test career termination date of Sydney 2024, decrypting press conference answers about him has become a full-time philological task.

We first burrowed into Steve Smith's banality at The Oval five weeks ago: 'It's nice to have an end date if that's the way you want to go, but ultimately we've all got to be doing our job, and for batters that's scoring runs. That's all of our jobs.' Now there is a perceived tension between coach Andrew McDonald's affirmation that he was 'not here to discuss David Warner' and Pat Cummins' hedging of 'you keep all options open'.

Yet it is perfectly possible for all these to be true, while there remains the further factor that no country is harder on numbers one and two than England: since the last home Ashes, the home team have gone through eight openers themselves. Warner was unlucky to suffer a leg-side strangle in the first innings at The Oval and a good ball in the second innings at Edgbaston, and then was excellent in demanding conditions at Lord's.

Would his understudy, Marcus Harris, rather puzzlingly preferred by Australia to the better-performed Cameron Bancroft, have proven so adaptable in similar circumstances? Would Test cricket of this summer's intensity be a suitable scenario to recast an opening partnership by relaunching a Test cricketer with three half-centuries in twenty-six innings? Harris, moreover, is an indifferent fielder, whereas Warner is an excellent one, as reliable this summer at slip (four catches) as Joe Root has been fallible (five misses).

So around we will go the next few days before, I suspect, winding up in the same place, with Warner best placed to walk out alongside Khawaja at Old Trafford. What we are guaranteed is that everyone will have an opinion.

17 JULY
EXTRAS

The little things count

In a series as close at the 2023 Ashes, little things are bound to matter. The littlest has, arguably, already had an influence. In England, they are called extras. In Australia, they have historically been called sundries, and still are on older scoreboards such as Adelaide Oval's.

However you describe them, cricket treats them like incidental expenses or petty cash. Which is odd, as byes, leg byes, no balls, and wides conceded all need to be compensated for, and often reflect a team's professionalism and preparation.

Byes, leg byes, wides and no balls loom all the larger in a series like this, where scores have generally been on the low side, with only one innings in excess of 400. Fully eight per cent of Australia's 1,850 runs in these Ashes have been English donations, 5.5 per cent of England's 1,809 from Australia.

Stuart Broad, moreover, cost himself Usman Khawaja's wicket at Edgbaston by overstepping when the batter was 112 going on 141, and rued it afterwards: 'It was a great ball, and it's very hard to put it at the back of your mind.'

England then lost by 43 runs at Lord's after surrendering no fewer than 74 extras, including 25 no balls and wides. One wondered at the time, in fact, whether all Bazball's big flourishes were at odds with England's snapping up unconsidered trifles.

But then, at Headingley, the hosts had a welcome outbreak of frugality: they bowled three no balls and no wides in the whole game, versus the tourists' twenty. And, like Australia in the first two Tests, they won despite scoring fewer runs off the bat in the game.

This went to an overall impression that, at Leeds, England played not just the better cricket but the tidier, particularly in becalming Australia's second innings at the point the tourists threatened to take the game away. In that truncated third day, they were visibly sharp, even relentless, in support of Chris Woakes and Mark Wood.

It may not have been an approach calibrated to reconnect with the players' innocent youths or to save Test cricket from its numerous existential threats, but it reflected the attention to detail that distinguishes quality teams.

Smart interceptions, speedy retrievals, throws over the stumps: we recognise these as contributions to the common weal even though they have no immediate numeric value. It is strange that the game doesn't nourish a like appreciation of things that do; sometimes, you suspect, teams tolerate extras as an implied boast that they do not sweat the small stuff.

But it reflected nothing of the kind when England bowled more than three times as many no balls and wides as Australia in the Ashes of 2021–22: it was indicative of nothing but the general shabbiness of their cricket. And twenty-four English no balls versus four Australian at Edgbaston was surely too many.

Australia's First Test thrift, meanwhile, almost certainly reflected atonement for their rustiness in the World Test

Championship final, where Pat Cummins twice cost himself wickets with too long a stride. Sloppiness round the front line is especially heinous now it is policed by the third umpire, and both over rates and bowlers' loads are so vigilantly policed. Ben Stokes presented a moving sight at Lord's as he toiled manfully over fifteen overs, but also bowled nine balls more than he needed, one of these costing him a wicket.

When Pat Cummins finally grudged Todd Murphy an over in the second innings at Headingley, he'd have been unimpressed that the young spinner, caught out by the end's slight gradient, started by overstepping. On the eve of lunch, at the end of a taut session, the avoidable error felt like a key concession: the English crowd greeted it with a lusty cheer; Australian hearts sank.

The challenge for England now will be to maintain standards as distractions mount, and fatigue and attrition take hold. They must also tighten those areas where they remain deficient. Australia have an abiding edge, for example, behind the stumps, where Alex Carey's twenty sharp dismissals have been smudged by only a couple of errors and twenty byes, while Jonny Bairstow has spilt a third of the chances to come his way and conceded forty-six byes.

Bairstow is fortunate Harry Brook came to his rescue at Headingley after Mark Wood took Mitchell Starc's top edge late on the third day when the game was in the balance. His hesitant immobility might not have proved so costly as it did when Khawaja nicked behind in the first over of Australia's second innings at Edgbaston, but another twenty runs or so would have left England stretching to make the match's highest score batting last. The task is at hand. Success this summer will be about taking as much as possible, but also giving as little.

The Fourth Test: Old Trafford

19–23 July 2023
Match drawn

MATCH REPORT

Rain men

Ben Stokes publicly scorns draws, but even he is powerless before the weather, and nowhere does weather quite like Old Trafford. For three days of the Fourth Test, England did not put a foot wrong, only to tread in a giant, spreading puddle that put paid to its chances of retrieving the Ashes. Australia was still 62 runs short of making England bat again with five second-innings wickets in hand when the final day was washed out altogether. It was hard to remember them playing so poorly on a pitch so blameless.

In truth, Australia's confusion was pre-existing, reflected in their picking an XI without a specialist slow bowler, even as England was strengthened by the exclusion of Robinson for Anderson. They then made a muddle of their first innings, with six batters getting to 30 and none exceeding 51, including Marnus Labuschagne and Steve Smith, who also burned reviews as their concentrations lapsed. Mitchell Marsh again looked the best equipped of the top order, striking the ball authoritatively in a 60-ball half-century. But Woakes bowled with control and variety to take five for 62. With Australia's Kookaburra, Woakes has been inclined to resemble a bowling machine; with England's Dukes, to paraphrase Woody Guthrie, this machine kills batters.

Over the next two days, Stokes' men set out to achieve a position of such crushing dominance as to obviate the need to bat again, and succeeded. Crawley, English cricket's preeminent delayed gratification, paid off, in the highest and freest innings of the summer: 189 in 182 balls, shimmering with twenty-one fours and three sixes—mainly off the same attack that in Australia had kept him to an average of 27—enjoying the pace on the ball, the speed of the outfield.

Early on, it was a battle. In his fourth over, Hazlewood had Crawley edging just short of slip and then turned around to be beaten on the outside; Crawley responded with a goose-stepping drive through mid-wicket. On 20, he was adjudged lbw to Green; he nervelessly reviewed, survived, carved Green square, and punched down the ground. When Head was thrown the ball, Crawley reversed for four and swept for six. When Cummins posted twin mid-wickets to Hazlewood, Crawley bisected and went fine of them. The long, barren stretches of Crawley's previous career fell away as a scurried two off Cummins brought him a 93-ball century, calling to mind Stokes' first principle of selection: 'We pick teams and players for what they can do on their best days.' On that second afternoon when England added 178 in twenty-five overs, in fact, Bazball seemed to go mainstream; it was every other approach that was the departure, everything else the variant; it was like learning that Bitcoin was now the world's reserve currency, that the Titanic had actually been a submarine. Cummins, meanwhile, was helpless to repair the damage to his own vessel, having no sooner plugged one leak and battened another hatch than it was borne down on by icebergs.

Even the pro tem number three pitched in, Moeen launching Crawley on his way in an easeful 121-run partnership in 152 balls. Crawley's liaison with Joe Root of 206 from 186 deliveries was not England's largest for the third wicket, but assuredly the fastest of its scale. In 2021–22, Root as captain had had the air of a careworn bus driver on a drably familiar route; now he resembled a young man in a convertible, wind in his hair, fun on his mind, foot pressing every now and again on the accelerator. Until defeated by a ball staying low, the attack held no terrors for him whatever.

On Crawley's dismissal, the whole Australian team queued to shake his hand in turn; given the chance, the crowd might have done so also. But England were not letting up. On day three, after Stokes and Brook had added a relatively sedate 86 in 132 balls, Bairstow jogged to 49 from 50, then sprinted a further 50 in 31. England's last wicket added 66 in 49, to which Anderson tossed in the loose change of 5 from 18 deliveries before being the last man dismissed. Might Stokes have declared earlier? Perhaps, but the spur of a single session's bowling followed by an evening's rest was just about ideal, and Wood struck with his second ball to remove Khawaja from the finest of nicks.

Warner outlasted Broad without convincing that this was other than a temporary stay; this time, after first tucking him up, Woakes seamed one away from a hesitant defensive bat. At last, with stumps in sight, Wood persuaded Smith to play a distressed hook and Head an anxious fend. Australia still needed 167 to make England bat again with six wickets remaining. But late that night, it began to rain. England would have heard it drumming on their windows with dread but no surprise.

Overnight pair Labuschagne and Marsh held England at bay most of the two hours possible on the third day, extending their partnership to 103 in 187 balls with some shrewd and measured defence that never quite descended into negativity. Labuschagne, after a barren few months, celebrated his second Test century abroad; Marsh celebrated simply being there, after a long first reservitude. The most threatening bowler proved to be Root, who almost had Labuschagne caught at slip from a mercurial arm ball, then had him caught at the wicket with some extra bounce. Green had just come together with Marsh when the boom of the weather fell, not to lift for 36 hours.

In the circumstances, there wasn't much to savour about Australia's retaining the Ashes. 'It's a bit of a strange one,' Cummins confessed. 'As a group [we're] proud that we've retained the Ashes, but it's off the back of not our greatest week … I don't think there will be huge celebrations.' Stokes, captaining in a draw for the first time, praised the cricket as he rued the outcome: 'We're always putting our front foot forward and trying to press the game as hard as we possibly could. As a captain, that's something that makes me very proud as a leader of the ten other guys out there. It's just unfortunate that we managed to get three hours in over the last two days … We were completely and utterly dominant throughout the hours of play we had. It's a shame, but, oh well.' The Oval was now his target; better weather, his prayer.

19 JULY

Day 1

The coming of Steve Smith and Marnus Labuschagne to these Ashes is becoming its juiciest non-story. They arrive at each Test with a trumpet blast of averages; they loom for a time with an ominous certainty; and somehow it is all staved off, adjourned to another day.

On the eve of this Fourth Test, the preconditions seemed to reach critical. Pat Cummins observed that Smith and Labuschagne 'had moved their hotel pillows into the nets'. They were observed there, heads together, speaking that peculiar cricket Esperanto of theirs, doubtless finishing one another's sentences. The arcana of batting is their shared delight, their creed and code.

Despite having restricted the Australian duo to one score of more than fifty this summer, England, at least for public consumption, remained superstitiously cautious. Asked about their form last week, Ben Stokes mumbled: 'You don't read too much into stuff like that against world-class players.' Moeen Ali almost indulged in prophecy: 'Great players are always due, and they are due some runs … As the opposition, you know it's around the corner for players like that.'

At stages on either side of lunch of this teasing, fluctuating first day at Old Trafford, that prudence looked well justified—if not quite a corner turned, perhaps a roundabout entered. But, again, England were able to manoeuvre Smith and Labuschagne into a cul-de-sac. The great and the world-class have something in common with the humblest village battler: it only takes one ball to get them out.

Both captains came to the toss with the short-term indicator (South Africa's dismissal for 151 on the first day last year) rather than the long-term trend (an average first-innings score of 386 in the last ten Tests) uppermost in their minds. When Cummins called incorrectly, Stokes threw the new ball to Stuart Broad, who defeated Khawaja's inside edge and hit his pads in front.

In his continuing head-to-head with Broad, Warner had a qualified success, by cannily spending twenty of the twenty-four balls of the bowler's opening spell at the non-striker's end. In his favour, Warner slotted a positive cut and a nimble pull, and oozed purpose at the crease and between the wickets. Then he seized the day a little too tightly, driving overeagerly as Woakes pushed the first ball after drinks across him.

When Smith hoisted Woakes' next ball high to long leg, English hopes also soared, only for Mark Wood to have come off the perimeter, and be unable to retrace his steps. No batter prospers without luck. Was this to be Smith's? He picked Broad off when the ball was too wide and too straight; ten minutes before lunch, he mowed Moeen for six. It looked like a day, and a surface, of which Smith could partake at his leisure.

Labuschagne settled also. In spite of his fussy geometry of blockhole etchings, he played with virtuous simplicity, defending primly in the V, leaving decisively to the off. His half-century partnership with Smith, in a fluent 71 deliveries, appeared a mere down payment. Labuschagne later idled while on 40 for twenty-four deliveries, without looking overly fussed, and then unfurled the sweetest of cover drives off Broad.

By then, however, Smith was out, beaten for pace by Wood in crab-walking ever further across his stumps. He immediately began gesturing with his left hand, technically to encourage the belief that the ball was missing leg stump, but also as if to ward off evil. On review, however, Wood's rapidity defeated Smith's denialism.

Labuschagne had just reached his second half-century in seventeen innings when he was also judged lbw, to Moeen, pushing outside the line of a ball that spun quite sharply, the review again corroborating the first impression. Labuschagne departed with his usual martyred air, hand to head, heart on sleeve. Nor was it quite what the team's selectors would have wanted, having elected to go without a specialist spinner.

The quid pro quo, of course, is that this Australian XI bats way deep, a solitary run short of having a top nine all with Test centuries. Travis Head again proved awkward to quell, and Mitchell Marsh hit the ball so hard that you feared for its remaining a sphere. Atoning for their relative passivity at Headingley, the Australians also ran enterprisingly all day, the stump mic eavesdropping on their characteristic locutions, from Warner's urgent 'Push, push' to Marsh's companionable 'Yeah, mate.'

But 92 from Smith and Labuschagne in 167 deliveries? It was, once more, almost certainly within England's budget, and a disruption to the Australian master plan of paving fast bowling's path with fat, flat-pitch hundreds. Eight for 299 was not an altogether unsatisfactory day's work, but in these conditions also represented runs forgone. Which is not what Australia would have wanted; nor, as summer began, what anyone would have expected from Labuschagne and Smith.

Stumps: Australia 1st innings 299/8 (Mitchell Starc 23*, Pat Cummins 1*, 83 ov)

20 JULY

Day 2

As Australia's cricketers contemplated the Ashes this summer, those who had been watching England's year of barnstorming spoke of a need to be prepared. There would be phases in the series where the home team would burst the bonds of accurate bowling and defensive field formations, and would appear to charge off with the game. In these circumstances, the team would simply have to keep their heads, stick to their core skills, and wait for the gradual restoration of equilibrium between bat and ball.

Such a time came yesterday afternoon. But as England piled on 178 in twenty-five overs between lunch and tea, it felt less like Australia was chasing the game than being dragged behind a chariot with knives on its wheels.

Viz the last ball of the thirty-eighth over. Mitchell Marsh had done well to restrict scoring to seven singles in his first eleven balls before rolling his fingers cannily over for his twelfth. This provided more time, it turned out, for Joe Root to squat for his speciality reverse lap, where he looks like a farmer shovelling hay over his shoulder. As the ball descended over the far side of the rope, Pat Cummins at mid-on was as much a spectator as everyone else.

Edgbaston had been a harbinger, but Australia there at least had had Nathan Lyon as a mildly tethering influence. Now there was no Lyon, and either too little method or too much. Bowlers were too straight then too wide, bowled to one side of the wicket then the other, struggled with their lengths, muddled their variations, and neglected the front line (delivering eleven no balls in 72 overs).

Fields were constructed, reconstructed, deconstructed, and destructed, their average life maybe three to four overs. There were twin deep gullies, multiple fly slips, and even multiple captains, with Steve Smith at slip semaphoring busily; later, he gave away three overthrows. Faced with a similar predicament, Victoria's government would simply have withdrawn from the Test; Australia had no such recourse.

In partnership first with Moeen Ali, then Joe Root, Crawley was a revelation, perhaps even to himself, although this was the innings that England had gone on thinking he was born to play—a century in a session in which his big shots made the space for his little shots to count. It was a Bazball without the manic edge glimpsed at Lord's, and both purposeful and judicious.

For all his lust for the booming drive, the shot of Crawley's that has really caught the eye this summer is the stroke, taken waist high, placed just in front of square leg to wrong-foot the field and/or turn the strike over. At one stage, Cummins posted two mid-wickets, which Crawley first bisected and then went finer by moving over to off stump. End of experiment; start of another.

Batters assuredly rode their luck: few have reviewed an lbw more profitably than Crawley (when on 20) before lunch. The first ball after lunch, Moeen punctured cover with a priceless drive, and then hit over the top of a grisly slice; Crawley drove headlong just wide of gully off Green, and then eased the next ball laconically down the ground.

Crawley greeted Travis Head with sweeps, oriental and occidental, and Moeen disposed of a full toss and then miscued a half-tracker that eluded an unsighted Cummins at mid-off. In the next over but one, Cummins mistimed his dive and spilled Moeen at mid-wicket.

It cost Australia only the skin on the captain's elbows, as Moeen fell soon after, although England's ersatz number three may never have made an Ashes contribution so crucial. The milestone of his 3,000th Test run reminded one that had his career coincided with Graeme Swann's, or had there been another specialist slow bowler capable of shouldering the bulk of the overs, Moeen might have been a top-order batter to be reckoned with.

Root made the most of the protective detail that Moeen had provided: Cummins, so successful against him, had just completed a spell. When Cummins did return, Root stood back and tall to handle the inevitable short stuff, while the scattered field could not stop Crawley driving and slashing Mitchell Starc through the 90s. Bodies have been wrapped in blankets and dumped in the Thames more tenderly than Crawley and Root treated one of Australia's most accomplished Test pace attacks.

And, of course, there was little else on offer, with no specialist spinner to take off the pace that Crawley so enjoys. As he drove Cummins down the ground either side of the stumps after tea, Crawley looked like a batter disposing of throw-downs; as he wellied Marsh into the crowd, he resembled a golfer teeing off.

Having made their statement, England had no need to repeat themselves. In the last session, they added 145 in 31 overs—progress that was almost leisurely by comparison. The Australian top-six batters, five of whom had exceeded 30 in their first innings, but none of whom had exceeded 51, looked on. Cummins, in his fifth Test of the summer, looked exhausted; Starc, who fielded manfully all day, went off feeling a shoulder. Behind Carey, as Labuschagne bowled the final over, reposed an unused protector in the spot usually reserved for the surplus helmet. It was like a fig leaf for Australian embarrassment.

Stumps: England 1st innings 384/4 (Harry Brook 14*, Ben Stokes 24*, 72 ov)

21 JULY

Day 3

'Is it cowardly to pray for rain?' was the title of a wonderfully droll account of the 2005 Ashes series. Today, the boot is snugly on the other foot, amidst a series where boots have been more or less constantly swapping.

Eighteen years ago, it was England who were desperate for the elements to help them preserve their two-to-one lead; now it is Australia who at Old Trafford need assistance towards the draw that would secure the Ashes for another two-and-a-half years at least.

Australia's series score line advantage hardly seems much consolation in this growingly one-sided Test, like an encouragement to Russian troops in Ukraine that, y'know, they won the earlier big one against the Third Reich. But it starts to matter now as, with Europe parched and alight, Manchester carries on doing its own thing meteorologically.

If the forecasts are fulfilled today, the fourth day will be the visitors' best of the match. That's because yesterday was in its own way a shambles—a politer shambles than the second day, perhaps, but as poor as the first day when Australian batters failed to finish what they had started. Twelve Australian innings have made it as far as 15 in this match; none have passed 51. The batters have been hunted, hounded, and harried to the brink.

Soft dismissals some, for sure. But soft dismissals often reflect earlier hardships. Take David Warner. He had escaped Broad around the wicket in the first innings, only to encounter Chris Woakes over the wicket; now Woakes again beat him on the outside as he felt for the ball. Pushing out a little further to meet the next ball, Warner dragged on.

When Warner was dismissed for 4 and 1 at Headingley, one hesitated to draw conclusions: early dismissal is an occupational hazard for openers, as it was for canaries in coalmines. There is something more concerning about his falling here for 34 and 28 after finding no sort of fluency at any stage. There were no smiles, whimsical or resigned, this time: Warner departed stonily.

Steve Smith is searching. The sages are observing his technique in the micro—the constant shiftings of his guard, the subtle nuances of his trigger movements. But the story is not in the what; it is in the why. Smith's greatly lauded 'problem solving' appears to have become his problem. He is like the man trying to get to sleep by turning first one way and then the other, adding and then subtracting pillows, counting sheep, breaths, runs, etc, and in doing so keeping himself awake.

Yesterday, Smith was not even booed as he came in, which some hereabouts probably think a breach of the spirit of cricket. When the third umpire (sensibly) adjudged a low edge of his not to have carried, there was neither on-field carry-on nor crowd disturbance; there was the sense, instead, that another chance would come, as was not the case in 2019, when every missed opportunity was accompanied by a gnashing of teeth.

Perhaps it is the real and present danger of Mark Wood's pace that is making the difference. He has certainly moved the dial on this series. At Edgbaston and Lord's, Usman Khawaja's batting had the gentle insistence of the tides; his defence was blasted open at Headingley, and his involuntary flinch yesterday resulted in the tiniest of edges.

Wood then dismissed Smith a second time in the match. Having had Smith looking for a short ball in the first innings, Wood suddenly let it go, and a hesitant hook was the result. Travis Head's name, meanwhile, is becoming a case of nominative determinism; he was defending it from Wood when the ball hit his splice.

For the day's first half, England had continued on their merrie old way, even if Stokes did cost his team time in indulging Jonny Bairstow's pursuit of a thirteenth Test hundred.

To be fair, Bairstow can hardly be accused of malingering, finding boundaries even when the perimeters were patrolled by all nine fielders, blatting Starc, Cummins, and Hazlewood into the crowd for six. Twice, amid general hilarity, he called for byes off Cummins and Green, challenging Carey to hit the stumps underarm.

If his place has never been openly under threat, Bairstow's mind has clearly been divided since Lord's. He continues glancing superstitiously over his shoulder at Carey every time he leaves his crease; had he salt, he would cast it.

The Headingley Test was Bairstow's least effectual in two years; few players on either side needed, and would have so embraced, the ensuing nine-day hiatus; he lit up on Thursday, a man refreshed, when he caught Mitchell Marsh, diving right, by far his stronger wing.

With the bat, he enjoyed the freedom of mission, the clarity of the deadline, and the support of the tail, which in the end was not quite enough to spirit him to a century. But as the innings ended, Bairstow hared in so swiftly to adopt his keeping gear that he only cursorily acknowledged the applause, almost passing Stokes as England's captain hurried out to warm up. Time to get going.

Four wickets in forty-one overs was a good recompense for England's efforts; a 162-run deficit for Australia is still daunting. So is praying for rain cowardly? A little. But as Yossarian observes in *Catch-22*, sometimes cowardice is the only sane response to an insane situation. And this series is proving deliciously insane.

Stumps: Australia 2nd innings 113/4 (Marnus Labuschagne 44*, Mitchell Marsh 1*, 41 ov)

22 JULY

Day 4

What goes up must come down, not least for batting averages. Careers arc. Powers fade. Appetites dull. Either that, or players would play for ever. Bowlers catch up, too, while captains get wise and critics hover.

The slightly odd aspect of the lull in the career of Marnus Labuschagne, which he arrested yesterday with an eleventh Test hundred after going without for seven months, is that none of the foregoing applied. Australia's number three was never obviously out of form; merely of runs, and perhaps rhythm also, the beat of his career since the last Ashes in England having been so relentless.

His 111 in four-and-a-half hours and 173 deliveries was Labuschagne at something like his best: calm, chanceless, soundly based, evenly paced. His 187-ball partnership of 103 with Mitchell Marsh has given Australia a hope of saving this Old Trafford Test match and thereby securing the Ashes, just as his dismissal as time ran short gave England a late lift, on a day when there was less cricket than hoped for but more than many expected.

Morning broke amid intense local rain and frustration to match, to the point where some seemed to expect Australia to be prepared to declare and obediently lose the game in compliance with the spirit of cricket. Alas, as the news ticker on Sky's fill-in programming showed, 'Start delayed', it was tempting to consider synonyms: 'Start derailed', 'Start deluged', or 'Start defunct'.

In the event, play was nearer than almost anyone imagined. Jimmy Anderson bowled the first ball just before 2.45 pm, with Jonny Bairstow coming up to the stumps to keep the batters crease-bound, and the lights doing their best to supplement the pale illumination.

But England found neither sideways movement nor variable bounce, nor even that much encouragement for Mark Wood: pace bowling suddenly felt like chopping wet logs. Rather, Labuschagne and Marsh batted with disarming freedom, the one moment of endangerment when Marsh hit up and under to the leg-side boundary, the ball dropping just wide of Moeen, the sweeper.

Otherwise, the crowd was subdued, and the over rate uninspiring: only a dozen in the first hour, despite neither appeals nor reviews. The ball needed replacing; the Bazball appeared to lose shape also.

This suited Labuschagne's mission. Just last December, after his tenth hundred, he was averaging a heady 61, in the process rivalling his boon companion Steve Smith. Then began a gradual stepping-down — not quite the *Sports Illustrated* cover jinx or the Colliwobbles, but appreciable nonetheless, reflected in an average of 33 in eleven Tests, and in the decline of his Test ranking from one to five.

There was, as observed, no particular pattern to his dismissals, nor an obvious technical fault to correct. Rather, Labuschagne seemed stuck in a perfectionistic loop — it can be tiring sometimes to watch him, such is the fierceness of his work ethic in the nets and the static electricity he emits even in repose.

Since nicking off first ball at Edgbaston, the 29-year-old has put together a string of starts in these Ashes, and each time succumbed to his first error.

More culpably, he holed out in the second innings at Headingley, and fell mutedly in the first innings here, causing his average to fade to 53. That's still more than Ricky Ponting and Mike Hussey—whose peak averages, by the way, were 60 and 85 respectively. But Labuschagne's record is less uniform, the salient discrepancy being between his averages abroad and away: he has been twice as effective in Australia as elsewhere.

To redeem that yesterday required some steady defence and some opportunistic offence. At 4.15 pm, the umpires decided arbitrarily that England could no longer bowl their pacemen. Moeen took the ball, with his usual varieties: some excellent deliveries, some dross.

Joe Root came on, and Labuschagne on quick feet lofted down the ground: a first six reduced Australia's deficit to less than 100, and a second propelled the batter into the 90s. Then came a dash of luck: an inventive seamer from Root took Labuschagne's outside edge, and zoomed past Crawley in close attendance at slip.

A scampered off-side single then brought Labuschagne only his second hundred in twenty offshore Tests. By the subdued celebrations, he displayed an awareness that his job was only half done; by his disconsolate response to being caught at the wicket by Bairstow, he acknowledged the continued risk to Australia. To reinforce it, Marsh (on 31) gave a half-chance to Harry Brook off Root in the same over.

The last day here, nonetheless, looks in serious peril. By the standard set at Edgbaston, where England felt they had morally won despite actually losing, having the better of a draw here would almost demand a national holiday. But everyone with a bit of cricket in their soul would leave at least a little disappointed:

Australia have been beaten in Manchester everywhere but on the scoreboard. In any case, Labuschagne will depart knowing that what goes down can also come up.

Stumps: Australia 2nd innings 214/5 (Mitchell Marsh 31*, Cameron Green 3*, 71 ov)

23 JULY

Day 5

Very little happens for the first time in cricket, or cuts only one way. Ten years ago, it was England who retained the Ashes at Old Trafford when rain ruined the Third Test with England three for 37 chasing 332, rendering it impossible for Australia to overtake their 2–0 lead.

I remember it well. The presentations occurred in a dark, largely empty ground, with Alastair Cook conceding that the weather hadn't 'been ideal' and that 'it was a slightly strange feeling' to resolve the series in such a way.

Not that there was much sympathy for the Australians at the time: lose two Tests by any margin, and you make yourself a hostage to fortune; it's only the generosity of the five-Test series that offers the possibility of redemption, which is mostly illusory anyway. In 141 years of the Ashes, only a team led by Bradman ever managed to turn around a two-nil deficit in the Ashes, because a Bradman is what it takes.

It was a similarly dismal way for custody of this instalment of the Ashes to be decided at Old Trafford yesterday, with the players who have played five weeks of such red-blooded cricket out of sight except in the highlights playing on a rain-smudged loop on the twin video screens, Bazbath supplanting Bazball.

The fantasy of two-all going to The Oval had been enchanting to both sets of fans; only the dimmest partisans so crave trophies as to be gratified by non-results.

Yet, as in 2013, the key to these Ashes lies not here in Manchester, in a Test that, for all England's dominant position, was not decided, but in those Tests that were concluded, however narrowly, in Australia's favour, at Edgbaston and Lord's.

England's batting has been brilliant to watch this summer, forcing Pat Cummins into some of the most defensive fielding formations an Australian captain can ever have set, with fewer slips than sweepers and nary a bat-pad catcher.

But that batting also let England down at crucial moments: on the fourth day at Edgbaston (when England, three-down and leading by 136, frittered away five for 100), and the third day at Lord's (when England, after being one for 188, were all out for 325 to trail on the first innings), Australia were clawing at the air when England offered them a share of a window ledge to hold onto.

To be fair, England learned from these setbacks. Marnus Labuschagne paid them a fair-minded tribute after play on Saturday night in batting away the inevitable question about Bazball, which as a description he said under-served England: at Old Trafford in particular, Labuschagne noted, Ben Stokes' team had 'adopted different styles', having 'taken the game on when it was time to take it on', but also on occasion 'sat back' and consolidated.

Alas for England, a little Australian edge in experience had already stood them in good stead through two nipping finishes, in the latter of which they played the match's second half with ten fit men.

It's the absence of that eleventh man, Nathan Lyon, that Australia has felt acutely at Headingley and Old Trafford—not least Pat Cummins, off whose captaincy Lyon's durability and economy has taken such pressure. It's no disgrace to say that Cummins was flummoxed by the challenge of managing an attack with first a junior slow bowler and then no slow bowler. Never mind Mike Brearley; it would have taxed Alan Turing.

Coming into this Test, Cummins professed himself renewed by his nine-day break. But he was like the man who returns from holidays only to find himself again feeling knackered after a few days back at his desk: his pace was down; his variation was minimal; his five full-length Tests in forty-six days a ridiculous regimen for a fast bowler, least of all one who also captains. And there is another starting in three days because, of course, we must have The Hundred.

Let's see what happens at The Oval, of course, but there is a good argument that England will end this series a better team than when they began, and that Australia will end it a little poorer. Certainly, the gap between the teams that yawned in 2021–22 has been decidedly narrowed. In that spirit, in fact, here's a tentative thought.

Convention dictates that the Ashes can only change hands if won outright, by a margin of at least one Test. Yet it is a convention of mysterious provenance, understood rather than codified. And I wonder whether it is quite fair, given that it confers a sizeable advantage before the teams even start, by effectively lending the draw a weighting that favours the holder: no clearer example could there have been than this Old Trafford Test.

Perhaps it is time to revisit this custom, to make provision for the Ashes to be shared. Looking out over a sad and sorry Old Trafford yesterday, it hardly felt as though Australia had quite 'won' the Ashes this summer, or that England had 'lost' them. On the contrary, it's been a series you'd be happy to have had go on forever.

It can't, of course. And we can be too fussy about these things, not least when we already compete for a trophy that never actually leaves its cabinet. As my friend Michael Atherton, in the context of umpiring, once averred: 'Life is unfair. Why should cricket be any different?'

But how to explain to the uninitiated The Oval Test's weird hybrid character, of being 'live' where the outcome of the series is concerned, but 'dead' in the context of the Ashes? I know cricket's not meant to make sense. But it might, on occasion, at least try to do so.

Stumps: No play

SCOREBOARD

Fourth Test: Manchester, 19-23 July 2023   **Toss:** England
Australia: 317 &214/5   **England:** 592

Match drawn

AUSTRALIA 1ST INNINGS

BATTING		R	B	M	4S	6S	SR
David Warner	c †Bairstow b Woakes	32	38	67	3	0	84.21
Usman Khawaja	lbw b Broad	3	19	22	0	0	15.78
Marnus Labuschagne	lbw b Ali	51	115	194	6	0	44.34
Steven Smith	lbw b Wood	41	52	65	5	1	78.84
Travis Head	c Root b Broad	48	65	97	7	0	73.84
Mitchell Marsh	c †Bairstow b Woakes	51	60	71	7	1	85.00
Cameron Green	lbw b Woakes	16	29	52	1	0	55.17
Alex Carey †	c †Bairstow b Woakes	20	49	78	2	0	40.81
Mitchell Starc	not out	36	93	121	6	0	38.70
Pat Cummins (c)	c Stokes b Anderson	1	4	11	0	0	25.00
Josh Hazlewood	c Duckett b Woakes	4	21	33	0	0	19.04
Extras	(b 8, lb 3, nb 3)	14					
TOTAL	90.2 Ov (RR: 3.50)	317					

Fall of wickets: 1-15 (Usman Khawaja, 4.6 ov), 2-61 (David Warner, 14.1 ov), 3-120 (Steven Smith, 29.2 ov), 4-183 (Marnus Labuschagne, 46.1 ov), 5-189 (Travis Head, 49.5 ov), 6-254 (Cameron Green, 62.1 ov), 7-255 (Mitchell Marsh, 62.5 ov), 8-294 (Alex Carey, 80.4 ov), 9-299 (Pat Cummins, 83.1 ov), 10-317 (Josh Hazlewood, 90.2 ov)

BOWLING	O	M	R	W	ECON	WD	NB
Stuart Broad	14	0	68	2	4.85	0	1
James Anderson	20	4	51	1	2.55	0	1
Chris Woakes	22.2	4	62	5	2.77	0	1
Mark Wood	17	5	60	1	3.52	0	0
Moeen Ali	17	1	65	1	3.82	0	0

ENGLAND 1ST INNINGS

BATTING		R	B	M	4S	6S	SR
Zak Crawley	b Green	189	182	272	21	3	103.84
Ben Duckett	c †Carey b Starc	1	6	10	0	0	16.66
Moeen Ali	c Khawaja b Starc	54	82	114	7	0	65.85
Joe Root	b Hazlewood	84	95	163	8	1	88.42
Harry Brook	c Starc b Hazlewood	61	100	163	5	0	61.00
Ben Stokes (c)	b Cummins	51	74	101	5	0	68.91
Jonny Bairstow †	not out	99	81	123	10	4	122.22
Chris Woakes	c †Carey b Hazlewood	0	1	5	0	0	0.00
Mark Wood	b Hazlewood	6	8	13	1	0	75.00
Stuart Broad	c & b Hazlewood	7	10	17	0	0	70.00
James Anderson	lbw b Green	5	18	42	1	0	27.77
Extras	(b 15, lb 9, nb 11)	35					
TOTAL	107.4 Ov (RR: 5.49)	592					

Fall of wickets: 1-9 (Ben Duckett, 2.1 ov), 2-130 (Moeen Ali, 27.1 ov), 3-336 (Zak Crawley, 56.5 ov), 4-351 (Joe Root, 61.1 ov), 5-437 (Ben Stokes, 83.1 ov), 6-474(Harry Brook, 91.6 ov), 7-486 (Chris Woakes, 93.1 ov), 8-506 (Mark Wood, 95.6 ov), 9-526 (Stuart Broad, 99.3 ov), 10-592 (James Anderson, 107.4 ov)

BOWLING	O	M	R	W	ECON	WD	NB
Mitchell Starc	25	0	137	2	5.48	0	1
Josh Hazlewood	27	2	126	5	4.66	0	2
Pat Cummins	23	0	129	1	5.60	0	4
Cameron Green	15.4	1	64	2	4.08	0	0
Travis Head	7	0	52	0	7.42	0	0
Mitchell Marsh	9	0	57	0	6.33	0	4
Marnus Labuschagne	1	0	3	0	3.00	0	0

AUSTRALIA 2ND INNINGS

BATTING		R	B	M	4S	6S	SR
Usman Khawaja	c †Bairstow b Wood	**18**	34	45	2	0	52.94
David Warner	b Woakes	**28**	53	79	3	0	52.83
Marnus Labuschagne	c †Bairstow b Root	**111**	173	270	10	2	64.16
Steven Smith	c †Bairstow b Wood	**17**	38	70	1	0	44.73
Travis Head	c Duckett b Wood	**1**	7	20	0	0	14.28
Mitchell Marsh	not out	**31**	107	157	4	0	28.97
Cameron Green	not out	**3**	15	12	0	0	20.00
Extras	(b 1, lb 2, nb 1, w 1)	**5**					
TOTAL	**71 Ov (RR: 3.01)**	**214/5**					

Did not bat: Alex Carey †, Mitchell Starc, Pat Cummins (c), Josh Hazlewood

Fall of wickets: 1-32 (Usman Khawaja, 10.2 ov), 2-54 (David Warner, 17.5 ov), 3-97 (Steven Smith, 32.3 ov), 4-108 (Travis Head, 36.1 ov), 5-211 (Marnus Labuschagne, 67.1 ov)

BOWLING	O	M	R	W	ECON	WD	NB
James Anderson	17	5	30	0	1.76	0	0
Stuart Broad	12	2	47	0	3.91	0	0
Moeen Ali	13	2	44	0	3.38	0	0
Mark Wood	11	0	27	3	2.45	1	0
Chris Woakes	12	5	31	1	2.58	0	1
Joe Root	6	1	32	1	5.33	0	0

Players show the way; spectators lose theirs

India's women's captain, Harmanpreet Kaur, is a gifted and combustible cricketer. During a one-day international against Bangladesh in Mirpur at the weekend ending in a tie, she responded to her dismissal by smashing down her stumps, remonstrating with the umpires, and gesturing to the crowd; at the presentation, she called the officiation 'pathetic'. She has since become the first female cricketer suspended for a level-2 offence under the International Cricket Council's code of conduct.

I know, I know, it's not the Ashes, before which all other cricket must bow. Maybe you could even spin it: women's cricket comes of age in achieving parity of misbehaviour with men. Except you'd be wrong, because Kaur's actions are vastly worse than almost anything you now see in elite men's cricket — these Ashes, which have been played in excellent spirit, being a case in point.

The deportment of both teams has been above reproach,

especially given the intensity of the cricket. Even the brief fuss of Lord's was contained. David Warner has been criticised, for smiling too much—a headline you'd hardly have predicted five years ago.

I'm old enough to remember tours of England when every other day involved opinings about Australian sledging. This summer, there have been just a couple of reported instances, in the form of send-offs—sledging at its most gormless, but also trivial. There have been more evidences of good feeling: having been smashed all over Lord's by Ben Stokes and Old Trafford by Zak Crawley, the Australians made a point of congratulating both. These incidents tend to go unreported because they are not news, which is a shame.

What's behind this sudden outbreak of reasonableness? Both teams are captained and coached by good men. Both teams are on the older side; they've been there, done that, and, as Michael Atherton noted yesterday, will in a few instances be doing it for the last time; better to look back in gratitude than in acrimony.

In a general improvement in the conduct of elite male cricketers, two other factors are probably at work. There is the comingling of players in franchise T20—it's notable that the one player in these Ashes who didn't get the memo, Ollie Robinson, is a stranger to these leagues.

There is also the bureaucratising of dissent, whereby players unhappy with umpiring have the right to appeal to the decision-review system—the Kaur incident is a reminder of how male players used to lose their minds over unfavourable decisions. Thanks to the foibles of the DRS, players still shake their heads walking off now and again, but this is in the nature of losing your temper with an ATM or being driven mad by your bank's hold music.

It's regrettable that the players have set a better example

this summer than the respective publics have. I was born here, have lived here, watched my first Test in England in 1985, and am on my seventh tour as a journalist. But whatever the reason—economic and cultural malaise, the collapsing standards of politics, the disinhibiting influence of social media, the twin banes of Brexit and Covid—this England feels a coarser, meaner, nastier place than even four years ago.

It was seen most clearly in the absurdly empurpled response to Alex Carey's stumping of Jonny Bairstow at Lord's, neatly spoofed this week in *Private Eye* with an advertisement for The Spirit of Cricket™: a 'subtle mix of beer, champagne, gin, whisky, cider and more beer … guaranteed to fill the cricket lover with patriotic fervour, a unique sense of justice and the unstoppable desire to share strongly held views about umpiring decisions with visiting Australian players.'

Theses could be written about the shades of opinion following this episode, between the woundedly sentimental (it's not cricket) to the severely professional (actually, it *is* cricket), but it was manna for the professional provocateurs who pander to our worst selves, and a mandate for real and virtual mobs to indulge their worst instincts.

Reports from Australian fans on the terraces have been dismaying. The Australian team has been more guarded, but Usman Khawaja spoke for many when he observed a week ago: 'Personally, if I am coming to the cricket and watching the cricket, I wouldn't want my kids to be around that. If I saw that I would 100 per cent make a complaint or just leave. I think some of the stuff can be pretty poor. Over at Edgbaston they were calling Travis Head a c… I'm like, I can't believe you can actually say that in a public domain anywhere.'

This courted the inevitable whataboutism: what about Australian crowds?! True enough, although that traditional unruliness has actually felt stifled in recent years by the excess of killjoy ordinances. English crowds have historically been relied on to police themselves, and have actually been good at it. But let's just say that they aren't as good as they were. Even at Lord's. Maybe especially at Lord's.

I'm reluctant to conclude that this is representative, by the way. It's as unfair to define a crowd by its stupidest members as it is a country by its stupidest citizens. This is a mistake, I think, that some of my countrymen at home have made: recourse has been too ready to the stereotype of the whingeing pom, just as it has the Aussie cheat.

So let's be clear about this: the vast majority of the followers of these Ashes in both countries have relished the cricket, evaluated it fairly, were disappointed by the soggy end at Old Trafford, and will make the best of The Oval. All the same, as unpopular as it will be to say so in these so-offended times, this otherwise excellent Ashes summer has been soured by a leering and bullying streak in English cricket that masquerades as banter but is no more than abuse — an abuse of the licence that the two countries have traditionally allowed themselves to poke fun at one another in cricket affairs. Maybe we could take a lesson from the players who've handled themselves so gracefully under a great deal more pressure.

Fifth Test:
The Oval

27–31 July 2023
England won by 49 runs

Farewell the trumpets

Some Ashes series have been let down by their finales. The 2023 Ashes would not be one of them. The Fifth Test at The Oval dawned in subdued fashion, but converged on a grandstand finish, with England carried to victory in a final spell of characteristic lethality by their most characterful cricketer, Stuart Broad. The teams that stood through the presentation ceremony afterwards, all passion spent, included several being seen on an English Test match field for the last time. Moeen Ali was completing his Cincinnatus mission. David Warner certainly and Steve Smith possibly were receiving their last boos in England, and it was hard to envision Usman Khawaja, Mitchell Starc, Josh Hazlewood, or perhaps even Pat Cummins himself returning.

If it was Cummins' last Test in England, it will not be one he remembers all that fondly, for sending England in after winning his first toss of the series was a puzzling decision, given the pitch's resemblance to the surface where Tim Paine disastrously did the same in 2019. Australia also made a poor start in the field against the busy bats of Ben Duckett and Zak Crawley, with Starc suffering after-effects of a fall on his shoulder at Old Trafford, and Cummins himself sporting a heavily bandaged left wrist (which proved to be fractured). But everyone was feeling the pinch after six gruelling weeks, including Moeen Ali, who damaged his right groin when setting off for a single in mid-afternoon as his partnership with Harry Brook was assuming menacing proportions.

Todd Murphy, thankfully recalled for Cameron Green, defeated Moeen's laboured swing, and Mitchell Starc continued his inconspicuously successful series with four wickets, including that of Ben Stokes, his off stump uprooted as he worked over-ambitiously to leg, and Brook, caught at slip after a spry two-hour 85. Hazlewood bowled both Root and Bairstow off inside edges, and it took a partnership of 49 in 54 balls between Woakes and Wood to guarantee England as many as 283. Australia, one for 61 at stumps, could congratulate themselves on a greater share of the day than had seemed possible after an hour.

The first hour of the second day could hardly have been more different: 21 runs, mainly extras, in twelve overs' stroke-less defiance from Khawaja and Labuschagne under a vault of cloud. Log cabins in the wilderness lined with tinned food awaiting the apocalypse have been erected with more expansive intent. There was a longer-term prospectus: batting was difficult now, but might be easier later. Neither batter would find out, though. On either side of lunch, Labuschagne was adeptly caught left-handed by a diving Root at slip off Wood after an innings of 9 in 82 balls, and Khawaja was beaten on the inside by Broad after a four-hour 47. Broad immediately nicked Head off, Anderson bowled Marsh off an inside edge, and Australia was again invested: in Smith we trust. He batted finely, but the inertia of Australia's top order had been hard to follow. Khawaja struck seven boundaries, which means that he eked out 19 from the other 150 deliveries he faced, so that England's control of the innings was never seriously challenged while he was there.

Australia were fortunate that electronic adjudication

reprieved Smith (on 42) as he dived for the crease just ahead of a fine pick-up and throw by substitute fielder George Ealham. Australia's tail hung in: Cummins stuck with Smith long enough to construct a meaningful partnership, and allowed Murphy his head in a sprightly one. Stokes temporarily lost his bearings, and Australia's number ten pulled three hearty sixes off Wood's predictable bouncers to ease Australia into an unexpected lead. But that lead vanished minutes into the third day when Crawley and Duckett took 13 from Starc's first over, and England were off on a day's almost casual run-making against an attack that, if not demob happy, never warmed to its task.

When Starc parted the openers after a breezy partnership of 79 in 104 balls, Stokes came in to a spontaneous and grateful standing ovation. His partnerships with Crawley (61 in 57) and Root (73 in 79) maintained England's momentum; Root went on to bat dreamily, including his party piece of the Sheffield Shovel over the third-man boundary, and Bairstow industriously, a meeting of method and task. Australia threw themselves about in the field, but rather wanted for inspiration and cohesion; it was a draining day for an already-drained team. England faltered only towards the close: when they might have batted Australia right out of the game, they gave away wickets a little light-heartedly. Broad alone could plead distraction: he crossed the boundary at the close to foreshadow his retirement on Sky. The thought of bowling his last ball in Test cricket against Australia 'filled me with joy', he said: at that stage, of course, he hardly knew the half of it.

There were stirring scenes the following morning when Broad resumed England's innings in the company of Anderson, on the latter's forty-first birthday. Would Anderson join in the farewell spirit? Ever the refusenik, he wasn't saying. Broad passed along through the Australian guard of honour, and pulled Starc for a valedictory six. Soon, they were sharing a last new ball for England—unmemorably, for it availed them little, on a day throughout which rain hung in the air. Warner and Khawaja presented full faces of the bat and greater urgency between wickets. Edges were beaten but untouched. Moeen battled his sore groin; Root, his part-timer's limitations. At England's party, the punchbowl had been yanked away. The status quo was disrupted only at the very end, when Wood clanged Khawaja's helmet hard—so hard as to necessitate the replacement of both headgear and ball. The umpires rummaging among the Dukes chose one seemingly darker, shinier, and harder than the pale and scathed item previously in use—this we know thanks to the superintendence of television and the pertinacity of Ricky Ponting in pointing it out the following morning every other over.

Cricket balls are capricious in their behaviours. Shiny ones can do nothing, scuffed ones a lot; they do not age uniformly; they feel different in the hand. So the equation shine = threat is inexact. The truth is that every ball change is a lottery. There is no pre-testing. The umpires are better placed than anyone to make the substitution, and do. The batters might have interdicted, as Labuschagne had at Old Trafford, but Khawaja was understandably more interested in his helmet. England bowled with what they were given. It all seemed a bit gratuitous when Australians began kvetching, tit-for-tat, about the 'spirit of cricket'. If a mistake was made, it was innocent; in this cricket life, there are enough deliberate infractions to complain about. It also made for an enthralling first hour of the final day, as Woakes had Warner caught at the wicket with one going one way, and Khawaja trapped on the crease with one going the other. Labuschagne threw his head back after edging Wood low to slip: for him, the Ashes had ended on a low note.

Smith and Head, however, demonstrated that batting was a viable concern, going run-for-run in a partnership of 95 from 147 balls, clarifying that victory was the Australian objective. As the sun pierced the morning cloud, they negotiated Wood and negated Anderson into the early afternoon. Smith had a second eccentric stoke of luck in the match when Stokes leapt at short leg to catch his inside edge, and in celebrating knocked the ball from his hand with his knee, reviewing sheepishly to no avail: the crowd sank into brooding. Boundaries after lunch were greeted with silence as Smith executed some idiosyncratic on-drives and Head preyed on width. At three for 264, Australia could glimpse victory just over the horizon: it would have been a remarkable achievement.

'Would have been' it remained: just then, Moeen, who had been rather hobbling around the field, abruptly turned a ball out of the rough, and Root caught Head at slip. Next over, Woakes got a ball to seam away, and Crawley caught Smith at slip. In the over after that, more spin from the rough had Marsh edging into his pad, and Bairstow adroitly catching the rebound: his series was arcing towards triumph. Four balls later, Starc followed a ball from Woakes across him, and Crawley again dived forward to take the chance: four for 11 from eighteen deliveries.

Suddenly, England could do no wrong. A drag-down from Moeen produced another wicket when Cummins' swipe rebounded off his thigh pad. Murphy shaped confidently, and Carey hit Moeen for a sweet straight six, but then came Broad, the pavilion at his back, the breeze at his beck, and Australia's left-handers his target, with a ball still so helpful that England stuck with it. In 2017–18, Broad had seemed finished; in 2022, he was almost compulsorily retired. But he had had the last word, and did for both Murphy and Carey, arrowing in at fourth stump, winning that little hint of wobble, and inducing edges behind.

Bairstow caught both, and the celebrations broke out.

Too soon? The whole match seemed too soon to be saying goodbye: where at the corresponding point of 2019 those Ashes had yet to begin, these Ashes were over, with almost two-and-a-half years till the next instalment. As if refusing to consent to the conclusion, the confetti cannons at the presentation ceremony failed to go off. There was no need for such palaver anyway: Tests like these are their own best advertisement.

27 JULY

Day 1

England probably had a morally successful first day of this Fifth Test. Who knows? We will have to ask them. On the scoreboard, the day was marginally Australia's, although, with the game having no potential influence on custody of the Ashes, there was a slight flatness to proceedings, a sense of it coming after the Lord Mayor's Show.

The dismal conclusion at Manchester has left us with a Schrodinger's Test, simultaneously dead (for the Ashes) and alive (for the series). It's perhaps more important for certain individuals, including Australians lately under pressure. For his part, Pat Cummins had a better day after his dire outing at Old Trafford: swifter with the ball and nimbler as captain, departing the Tesla autopilot field placings he had adopted this summer in favour of more orthodox formations, with multiple slips, and sweepers on only one side.

David Warner, by contrast, led a troubled life, dropped on 0 down the leg side, popping up a catch to where short leg might have been on 21, and nicking just short of the keeper on 23. He was just looking back at a tough period when Chris Woakes tapped him on the other shoulder, inducing a tame nick to slip. We have become used to saying that Warner has one more chance; now, literally, this series at least, he does.

England, however, should be the more dissatisfied, failing to hold Australia accountable for their lacklustre bowling start, when the tourists gave away the opportunity to bat in the first innings after winning the toss, were wayward with the new ball and listless in the field, missing chances from both openers in consecutive overs.

Neither English opener made Australia pay, though, and Root's absent-minded drag-on left England three for 73—which Australia could consider a reasonable morning's return. Root has looked in cracking form this summer, but has, like Australia in the first innings at Old Trafford, left some runs out there.

Had Carey held an outside edge from Brook (5) soon after, England would have been four for 79, but the Australian keeper chose the wrong day to have his patchiest performance of the series, troubled by that post hoc swing unknown in Australia.

Having also nicked through the vacant fourth slip, Brook then settled into his attacking groove, and what a powerfully rhythmic sight he is in full flow, with all the uncloudedness of youth. At lunch, England were three for 131 from 26 overs: it felt like an entire Test match in the session.

On drive, straight drive, cover drive, back cut: no boundary felt safe while Brook was there. Mostly memorably of all, his pick-up six off Marsh and his hooked six off Cummins, where Brook appeared to anticipate the shorter ball, were cases not so much of technique as of telepathy.

Australia might profitably have bowled short more often to Brook afterwards, but did not seem game to try—that's the effect of decisive stroke play. Nobody on either side has faster hands or eye for length than England's number four: he could only go deeper in his crease if he took guard behind his stumps.

But the day rather lost shape when, in the early afternoon,

Moeen strained a right groin and, rather than seek treatment, remained at the crease to slog on one leg: commendably determined, but also a little pointless, and in two senses counterproductive, costing the batters the capacity to get off strike, and placing Moeen in danger of exacerbating the injury.

There followed twenty minutes of chaos and calculation, with Moeen helping himself to a couple of hearty sixes, and Cummins dispersing his fielders. Then Cummins remembered he had a slow bowler, as he had not had at Old Trafford, and Todd Murphy defeated Moeen's hazy waft. Moeen then did not field: what is probably his final Test has started poorly.

At Old Trafford, England had exhibited a new knack for when to surge and when to sit back; in mid-afternoon, that aptitude rather deserted them. First Stokes, then Bairstow, then finally Brook attacked balls they could have defended or left, and England rather surrendered four for 28 in nine overs. England's stroke play would not have been out of place towards the end of an innings in a one-day international. Remember those? They used to be all the rage …

England won the corresponding Test here four years ago after scoring 294 on being sent in, but that seems another aeon ago, when ramps were something you drove up, and the spirit of cricket was kept for rubbing on bruises. All to the good, of course: this was an entertaining, at times absorbing, day of Test cricket: hard to complain about eleven wickets, 344 runs at 4.3 an over, five dropped catches, five sixes, and no overs lost to rain despite portentous skies.

Yet how much more appealing Bazball would be if England didn't behave like a celebrity expecting a round of applause every time they walk in the room. Viz England Cricket Board chairman Richard Thompson's preposterous hymn of self-praise on Radio 4 yesterday: in light of how England have 'reinvented the way Test cricket has been played now', Thompson would be calling on the International Cricket Council for 'schedules to be more flexible' in the light of the 'strange eventuality' at Old Trafford.

Errr, the 'strange eventuality' was rain in Manchester. Not that strange, surely. And it's the ECB, not the ICC, who have shoehorned the Ashes into forty-five days this summer, rendering an inflexible schedule rigid.

Some perspective, please: while Ben Stokes' team have been wonderfully watchable this summer, they have helped their own Test cricket, nobody else's. By acquiescing spinelessly in the ICC's next financial distribution, furthermore, the ECB are as guilty as any board of sabotaging international cricket. They should shut up, count their money, and spare us their hypocrisies.

Stumps: Australia 1st innings 61/1 (Usman Khawaja 26*, Marnus Labuschagne 2*, 25 ov)

28 JULY

Day 2

Another day; another Test match too close to call, after a morning, afternoon, and evening at The Oval that unfolded like a pitched battle, with phases of stalemate, breakthrough and regrouping, as Australia's first innings more or less cancelled out England's, albeit at a wholly different tempo.

No plan, reputedly, survives contact with the enemy, and Australia's proved no exception. As Usman Khawaja and Marnus Labuschagne eked 21 runs out of the first hour under low cloud and in dim light, their objective was clear: attempt to put back into the game the time England had taken out the previous day, mindful that batting would become easier in the afternoon as bowlers tired and the ball softened.

These were touch-and-go conditions, for sure. Khawaja glanced a boundary when Anderson's in-swinger got too straight; Khawaja was beaten when Anderson's away-swinger channelled fifth stump; he found fielders with crisp shots, and could find no force in gaps. But as Labuschagne also sank into introspection, both batters found themselves isolated, almost in separate and parallel games.

Mike Brearley tells a story of sitting with a group of former greats as a fast bowler worked over an English opener. The agony continued, over upon over, until at last the paceman took a spell, whereupon it was agreed that the batter had done well to outlast his opponent. The one note of demurral came from Sir Leonard Hutton. 'Aye,' said. 'Mind you, a good batter would've bin at t'other end.'

Labuschagne could not find a way to get there, nor Khawaja to engineer it. He faced 82 balls, 31 from the joltingly rapid Wood, one of whose deliveries knocked Jonny Bairstow off his feet.

In Wood's tenth over, Labuschagne might have scuttled a single to Stuart Broad, a little deep and a little less limber than he used to be at mid-on; Khawaja was unbudging, even turning his back slightly.

Bairstow was also unbudging a few balls later when Labuschagne nicked one, but Root timed his dive to the left perfectly: though he has shelled some straightforward ones lately, this was probably the catch of the summer.

Smith immediately drove soothing consecutive boundaries down the ground from Anderson, and otherwise looked of a different quality from anything else on show. 'The Oval', where he averages in the vicinity of 100, might be carved on his heart like 'Calais' on Mary I's. But England could work around him, and made the post-lunch session their own with perhaps their best bowling, fuller and to more or less conventional fields, of the series.

Bowlers have a variety of demeanours as they return to the end of their marks: grim, relaxed, solemn, detached. James Anderson's inscrutable walk back is almost a continuation of his trim and economical action.

I am partial to Broad's: unfailingly cheerful, like a man on a brisk walk down a familiar country road, lightly on the balls of his feet. He'll have a chat to the non-striker, to mid-off, to the umpire (often enough about the condition of the ball); he'll look up at the scoreboard and the video screen; winding up spectators is a speciality. Seizing the first over after the break, he was almost jogging back, so eager was he for the fray: he had a ball suddenly doing tricks, a crowd bubbling, and a left-hander in Khawaja to prise open.

When Kumar Dharmasena granted him an lbw against Khawaja, upheld on review, Broad stayed for a yarn, and clapped the umpire on the shoulder companionably a couple of times.

Twice he beat Travis Head on the outside, locked eyes with him, studied the replay on the way back, nodded his head, clapped his hands, and polished the ball with an extra flourish. Head was almost stationary as he nicked the next.

After the austerity of the first session, a flash of colour, movement, and cheer. Marsh arrived in the pink of form, and Bazballed a six over Broad's head. Broad looked a bit miffed, then appreciative. Bring it on.

In the event, Broad's old mucker Anderson worked one through Marsh's unpadlocked gate, and Root coaxed Carey into an indiscreet drive. When Starc top-edged a cramped pull shot from Wood, Australia had lost six for 94 in 30 overs — more a general subsidence than a collapse, but a gaping opportunity for the hosts.

It was not quite England's fault that it went unseized. When he was 42, Smith careened back for a second run on the arm of substitute George Ealham, unknown to fame but grandson of a splendid fielder for Kent. Ealham's throw, skimmed over the square, was brilliant; the decision, to be frank, was not, tediously searching for the skerrick of a smidgeon of a scintilla of doubt.

But there was all of Smith in the dive to save himself: perfectly timed, fully elongated, bat-holding arm telescoped ahead of him. He can't practise diving for the crease, surely? Strangely, it's almost plausible that he does.

This proved the day's hinge-point: had the decision gone

England's way, Australia would have been 90 runs short with only a couple of tail-end wickets remaining and the new ball due. As it was, Smith and Cummins extended their partnership to 54 in 103 balls. Nor did Stokes' plan against Australia's tail survive contact with the enemy.

Why have Wood pitch a 13-over-old ball halfway down the pitch with two men back and no slips to a batter averaging 10 in Test cricket when a fuller length had been so successful all day? Todd Murphy swivelled into three pull shots, all of them for six, and shaped so well that Australia secured the lead. Stokes ended the day on a more characteristic note, catching his opposite number at long-on with ursine strength and immense presence of mind. But the best in this match may be to come.

Stumps: Australia 1st innings 295 (Steven Smith 71, Usman Khawaja 47, 103 ov)

29 JULY

Day 3

There were two teams at The Oval yesterday. One of them was playing cricket; the other was ... well, trying very hard to play cricket, but could probably not have put their finger on how or to what end. England tackled the third day of the Fifth Test with plan and purpose. For a team that began in the lead, in the series and on the first innings, Australia approached their task with an uneasy fatalism.

Their hard-won innings lead of 12 runs lasted precisely six deliveries, erased by three boundaries in Mitchell Starc's first over. Australia's storied attack could, again, then make nothing of Ben Duckett and Zak Crawley—the very particular challenge of countering a short, left-handed, back-foot, closed-face batter and his towering, right-handed, front-foot, full-face partner playing the bowling on its merits rather than the bowlers' reputations.

The attempt to keep to a single off-side sweeper soon went by the board, as Mitchell Starc and Josh Hazlewood struggled to bowl to one side of the wicket. Not until Pat Cummins took up the ball himself were Australia able to exert any control at all, and he executed one virtuoso act, fielding off his follow-through and hitting the non-striker's stumps direct.

Otherwise, one could hardly miss the comparison, almost the

ideological clash, with proceedings a day earlier, when Australian batters had been confined to 41 runs off the bat in 26 pre-lunch overs—testament, it must be said, to some fine bowling combined with helpful overhead conditions versus a pitch now at its best under clear skies.

It hardly does the event justice to report that Stokes came out to bat at number three. As a proclamation of potency, it was received round The Oval like an arrival of Maximus bearing a Bazball aquila. ('Are you not entertained? Is this not why you're here?')

In fact, Stokes rather shied away from triumphalism. He batted accordingly—like a proper number three consolidating an early advantage, reading the game and his opponents, sensing that by mid-afternoon he would have them pretty much where he wanted.

Stokes' all-round future is in the balance. He will finish this series having bowled only twenty-nine overs, twelve of them off the reel at Lord's. But it's arguable he is a more natural number three than Ollie Pope, technically and temperamentally. His combination of bat, body, and willpower in defence has a legionnaire's impassability.

It was his predecessor and pal Joe Root who really took the game from Australia, in an innings studded with Bazball cameos (a ramp here, a reverse lap there), but more like previous models of his batting. First, there was a reminder of the breeziness of 2015, where he seemed to be 20 from 10 in every innings before you had time to blink, and went on to be player of the series. Later, came the supremely controlled Root of 2021, where every run looked like a down payment on a hundred, of which he made six in a year.

Root is not considered part of the long roll call in this game who may be playing their last Ashes cricket: he is only thirty-two, and it is easy to imagine him batting here in four years' time. But he has grounds for motivation. His non-Ashes average is 14 runs greater than his Ashes average, and he seems increasingly to regard himself as a work in progress: he has hit fifteen sixes in 2023 already versus 28 in the eleven years preceding. Here was reassurance, at any rate, that Root has not sacrificed avidity to creativity. It took a ball from Todd Murphy to spin sharply and stay low to puncture his defence.

At length came Jonny Bairstow to do Jonny Bairstow things, for there can be few better equipped to take a game on at four for 222, creating a sense of urgency even where none exists, repaying some if not all of the faith that England has shown in him this summer before he, Chris Woakes, and Moeen Ali perished a little lazily to Starc. That England batted all the way down to their last and oldest pair suggests, in fact, that they might have liked a few more runs on what remains an excellent pitch.

These came as late breaks. Otherwise, the day had a festive, even reminiscent, feel in the crowd. Never mind the Australians of 2005, whose Oval Test was inevitably revisited by Sky during the day; Cummins' looked like the Australians of 1985, being gorged on by Gooch and Gower on a balmy Kennington afternoon, overlooked by a venerable pavilion and the sadly endangered gasometers.

Cameos: an hour after tea, Cummins briefly had a field for Hazlewood of six men on the fence, no slips, no gully, and no point, literally and philosophically. Hazlewood hit Root's front pad, and before realising it had taken an inside edge gave a cry that sounded more like an appeal than a cry of pain. Later, he was unable to make ground to Moeen's top edge at fine leg, which the crowd did not let him forget.

Nothing, mind you, was cheered more lustily than Anderson's last-over sweeps and successful review, completing another jumbo pack of enterprise and entertainment, with nearly 400 in a day's play leavened by only two maidens. The Australians, in fact, have bowled fewer maidens than taken wickets this series. It is not even close: 34 to 84. Yesterday wasn't close either.

Stumps: England 2nd innings 389/9 (Stuart Broad 2*, James Anderson 8*, 80 ov)

30 JULY

Day 4

'Eng Need 10 Wickets To Win.' Up it went on the giant video scoreboard of the Finn Stand after twenty minutes of the fourth day of this Fifth Test, a helpful guide to the uninitiated as the home team set about their task of squaring this ever-so-close Ashes series.

Not, you'll notice, 'Aus Need 384 Runs to Win.' Only England's task warranted monitoring. Limited imagination? Subtle parochialism? Outright hubris? Granted, it was not the outlandish 'England 500–1' that blazed across the Headingley scoreboard in 1981 as that team reached its nadir; but, still, stranger things have happened in cricket, as England proved last year in its succession of death-or-glory chases. Hell, stranger things have happened this summer.

'Eng Need 10 Wickets to Win': and so it remained at 2.45 pm, as the rain that had concentrated over The Oval for much of the day finally burst, with Australia's target having been substantially reduced by the combined efforts of David Warner and Usman Khawaja.

Their best opening partnership of the series had by then become their first three-figure stand since March last year: 135 from 38 overs. All that could make the prospect of the last day here more tantalising is if the Ashes were on the line; as it is, there's a sizeable gap, at least in historic perception, between two-all and three-one.

The day began with the air of a benefit gig for Stuart Broad, saluted on potentially the last day of his England career with a guard of honour and a juicy bouncer, hooked into that same Finn Stand.

Still, when James Anderson became the last wicket, there was just the slightest feeling that England had left Australia something to grasp at by Bazballing away their last five wickets for 35 in nine overs. Sunday's 110-run partnership of Joe Root and Jonny Bairstow should really have put this match beyond the visitors' reach; why such haste at the back end of England's innings when there were more than two days' cricket to go?

Conditions boded ill for the Australian chase, the clouds closing in but the floodlights ensuring play, while rain on the radar formed a pincer around The Oval that declined to close. In the event, England's bowlers were sloppy and found negligible sideways movement, to the point that James Anderson, gifted the new ball on his birthday by Ben Stokes, was looking at it after a few overs as though at a toy for which the batteries had not been included.

Around Khawaja and Warner was also a tone of greater urgency, in contrast to the dilatory early phases of Australia's first innings, at one stage finding the boundary thrice in succession: Warner down the ground from Woakes, Khawaja down the ground and through cover off Anderson. Khawaja toe-ended an extravagant pull off Broad into the covers, but the intent was clear.

As Stokes fortified his off-side field, Moeen Ali limped around it. Handicapped by that sore groin, Moeen struggled to impart his usual revs, although he gave England its closest glimpse of a wicket, Warner (on 19) being so nonplussed by a waist-high full toss that he neglected to hit it to kingdom come and merely miscued into space.

The crowd, after its morning salaams for Broad and natal-day salute for Anderson, was distracted and subdued; the fates remained untempted and undisturbed. At one point, in consecutive overs, Stokes and Root superstitiously swapped the bails at each end à la Broad; at his end, Khawaja fastidiously swapped them back. Expect allegations of bail tampering: Piers Morgan will probably call it Bailgate.

A thumbs-up from Warner to Khawaja for the 50-run partnership; a pat on the back from Khawaja to Warner as the pair went in to lunch at none for 75. And afterwards, though England tightened, the pair went at a run-a-minute — probably drab by Bazball standards, but by Australian rates of progress this summer, a veritable frolic.

There were alarums when Joe Root bowled into the rough around the left-handers' off stump — a Warner gambol down the pitch hastily aborted, a Khawaja nick between slip and keeper. But three boundaries came from the bowler's last over: useful he may be, but Root is stand-in for a better spinner. Warner smiled wolfishly after Anderson delivered him a head-high full toss, which he deftly deflected to third man, then struck a once-familiar pose in lofting the same bowler down the ground.

Mark Wood's belated advent in the 33rd over tugged Khawaja into some French cricket postures, and a blow on his helmet would have set his ears ringing. Once again, one was thankful for the durability of modern headgear: what took a chunk from the ball would have taken quite a chunk from Khawaja's head.

In the over before drinks, Khawaja tiptoed past 5,000 Test runs, 2,114 of those at 62.17 since he returned to the colours just over eighteen months ago. As play was called off at 4.48 pm, spectators could catch a last glimpse of 'Eng Need 10 Wickets to Win.' Australia, meanwhile, now need 249 runs.

Stumps: Australia 2nd innings 135/0 (David Warner 58*, Usman Khawaja 69*, 38 ov)

31 JULY

Day 5

At 6.25 pm, a milky evening light bathed The Oval, and a breeze stiffened the flags atop the pavilion behind Stuart Broad as he ran in. A fleeting thought: why was he retiring? Perhaps because life could hardly get better than this.

A last left-hander for his delectation: Alex Carey's outside edge carried through to Jonny Bairstow. Amazing scenes! Glorious memories! And after twenty-four of a possible twenty-five days, Australia and England ... had played one another to a standstill.

No decision, then, though perhaps a shared moral victory, insofar as both teams stuck fast to their respective methods, England playing a vivid, expansive, sometimes electrifying cricket, Australia a game less volatile, more orthodox, and occasionally downright dogged. England scored at 4.74 an over, Australia at 3.32, and the lesson is that both ways can work.

The day dawned exactly as one would wish, with every result possible. Australia was well placed to hoist England by their chasing petard and come by their first series win in England in twenty-two years. England, as Philomena Cunk would say, stood at a fork in their crossroads, wondering how to reconcile vibes with victory. All that was missing were the Ashes. Imagine, for a moment, had they been at stake.

For much of the morning, rain felt minutes away and edges in constant peril: Chris Woakes beat David Warner on the outside and Usman Khawaja on the inside in a wonderfully controlled spell. Mark Wood sent a bouncer so far over Jonny Bairstow's head that the keeper could have stood on his own shoulders and failed to reach it. Next ball, however, Zak Crawley pocketed Marnus Labuschagne's nick at second slip, and Steven Smith's vagrant bat then just saved him from lbw.

As has often occurred in these Ashes, there emerged an esoteric controversy, fuelled by television, about the replacement ball: had it been too new? Blurry photographs were reproduced, data cited, investigations demanded, although perfidious Albion had destroyed the evidence by bowling with said ball. Cunning!

And yet, and yet. The ball still needed to be swung, which was mainly down to the skill of Woakes and Broad—Anderson, the greatest swing bowler of his generation, obtained nothing like the same assistance. The conditions also needed to be helpful, which was the almighty's prerogative—on another day, you could have changed the ball every over to no effect. Nor was the change entirely advantageous for England, for sometimes the ball did too much.

In any case, no sharp practice was demonstrable; the decision was in the hands of the umpires. While all this was going on, furthermore, Smith and Head were proving batting to be perfectly possible, even enjoyable: the pitch, after all, has done nothing for five days but improve. In the half-dozen overs after Woakes took a breather, the pair profited by 35 runs.

Yet we'd have gone on debating this slight zephyr in a reservoir-sized teacup had it not been superseded by Ben Stokes' catch that wasn't—and clearly wasn't, joining the annals of catches spoiled by premature celebrations (Gatting missing Border at Lord's in 1985; Gibbs missing Waugh in 1999, etc).

Rain allowed three hours for commentators and English supporters to brood over the potential cost of this gaffe: one noted that premature celebration has been an English tendency all summer, from the end of day one at Edgbaston to the end of day three at Old Trafford. And when play resumed at 4.20 pm with 47 overs remaining, Australia's objective (146 runs) looked decidedly more straightforward than England's (seven wickets) — the more so when Smith cover drove and pulled Woakes for militant boundaries.

Just then, however, a resumption of Head's old susceptibilities to off-spin, and a sharp catch by Root off Moeen, opened an end, which sometimes is all it takes. It was the first of five Australian wickets to fall for 30 runs in 47 balls, providing Crawley with his eighth and ninth catches of the series — his fielding has been almost as valuable as his batting this summer.

The crucial wicket, of course, was Smith, ominously sure for nearly two-and-a-half hours, until he defended faultily; the crucial bowler was Woakes, on his way to a well-deserved series award. It's ten years since Woakes made his Test debut on this ground, and was unbeaten on 17 when the umpires called the players in with England five wickets down needing only 21 runs for victory.

History since has seemed to toy a little with this admirable cricketer. Would he ever be a full-fledged Ashes winner? Before his recall for Headingley, he had only twice played in Test wins against Australia, contributing meagrely to each. His 19 wickets at 18, along with useful runs and a cool temper, have filled that gap in his career.

Still, Australia did not capitulate. Carey drove Moeen over the top for six; beaten monotonously by Broad outside the off stump, Todd Murphy flicked him over the top and swivelled into a stylish pull. Then, one last glimmer of Broad the gamesman, swapping the bails at the non-striker's end in a way that is bound to start a fad, but here did the trick again.

'What Test cricket needed,' pronounced Ben Stokes afterwards with clear satisfaction. It was tempting to assent. The 2023 Ashes certainly contained classic matches, and imperishable passages of play, mainly from the hosts: Stokes' assault at Lord's, Wood's insurgency at Headingley, Crawley's blitz at Old Trafford.

But, at risk of pooping the party, nor could one ignore the context. This was an Ashes series, not an Ashes summer. Australia have shoehorned six Tests into 54 days; England, six into 60. Australia now does not play its next Test until 14 December; England, not until 25 January.

Hours before the day began, one team beat another in Dallas, concluding a fortnight of T20 funded largely by Indian capital and principally sponsored by an online betting company; today, one team plays another in Nottingham to commence The Hundred, which the England Cricket Board will in due course try selling to similar corporate interests. Viva the Ashes! Long live Test cricket! That might be the most premature celebration of all.

Stumps: Australia 2nd innings 334 (94.4 ov) — end of match

SCOREBOARD

Fifth Test: The Oval, 27–31 July 2023   **Toss:** Australia
England: 283 & 395   **Australia:** 295 & 334

England won by 49 runs

ENGLAND 1ST INNINGS

BATTING		R	B	M	4S	6S	SR
Zak Crawley	c Smith b Cummins	22	37	62	3	0	59.45
Ben Duckett	c †Carey b Marsh	41	41	58	3	0	100.00
Moeen Ali	b Murphy	34	47	100	3	2	72.34
Joe Root	b Hazlewood	5	11	12	1	0	45.45
Harry Brook	c Smith b Starc	85	91	125	11	2	93.40
Ben Stokes (c)	b Starc	3	16	18	0	0	18.75
Jonny Bairstow †	b Hazlewood	4	14	16	0	0	28.57
Chris Woakes	c Head b Starc	36	36	63	4	1	100.00
Mark Wood	b Murphy	28	29	40	5	0	96.55
Stuart Broad	c Head b Starc	7	5	6	1	0	140.00
James Anderson	not out	0	3	8	0	0	0.00
Extras	(b 9, lb 7, nb 2)	18					
TOTAL	**54.4 Ov (RR: 5.17)**	283					

Fall of wickets: 1-62 (Ben Duckett, 11.6 ov), 2-66 (Zak Crawley, 12.4 ov), 3-73 (Joe Root, 15.3 ov), 4-184 (Moeen Ali, 33.3 ov), 5-193 (Ben Stokes, 38.3 ov), 6-208 (Jonny Bairstow, 41.6 ov), 7-212 (Harry Brook, 42.3 ov), 8-261 (Mark Wood, 51.3 ov), 9-270 (Stuart Broad, 52.5 ov), 10-283 (Chris Woakes, 54.4 ov)

BOWLING	O	M	R	W	ECON	WD	NB
Mitchell Starc	14.4	1	82	4	5.59	0	0
Josh Hazlewood	13	0	54	2	4.15	0	0
Pat Cummins	13	2	66	1	5.07	0	0
Mitchell Marsh	8	0	43	1	5.37	0	2
Todd Murphy	6	0	22	2	3.66	0	0

AUSTRALIA 1ST INNINGS

BATTING		R	B	M	4S	6S	SR
Usman Khawaja	lbw b Broad	47	157	237	7	0	29.93
David Warner	c Crawley b Woakes	24	52	74	3	0	46.15
Marnus Labuschagne	c Root b Wood	9	82	118	0	0	10.97
Steven Smith	c †Bairstow b Woakes	71	123	225	6	0	57.72
Travis Head	c †Bairstow b Broad	4	5	8	1	0	80.00
Mitchell Marsh	b Anderson	16	28	31	1	1	57.14
Alex Carey †	c Stokes b Root	10	23	29	1	1	43.47
Mitchell Starc	c Duckett b Wood	7	18	24	0	0	38.88
Pat Cummins (c)	c Stokes b Root	36	86	148	4	0	41.86
Todd Murphy	lbw b Woakes	34	39	54	2	3	87.17
Josh Hazlewood	not out	6	7	10	1	0	85.71
Extras	(b 17, lb 12, nb 1, w 1)	31					
TOTAL	103.1 Ov (RR: 2.85)	295					

Fall of wickets: 1-49 (David Warner, 16.5 ov), 2-91 (Marnus Labuschagne, 42.5 ov), 3-115 (Usman Khawaja, 51.5 ov), 4-127 (Travis Head, 53.4 ov), 5-151(Mitchell Marsh, 60.4 ov), 6-170 (Alex Carey, 67.5 ov), 7-185 (Mitchell Starc, 72.5 ov), 8-239 (Steven Smith, 89.6 ov), 9-288 (Todd Murphy, 101.2 ov), 10-295(Pat Cummins, 103.1 ov)

BOWLING	O	M	R	W	ECON	WD	NB
Stuart Broad	20	5	49	2	2.45	0	0
James Anderson	26	9	67	1	2.57	0	1
Mark Wood	22	4	62	2	2.81	1	0
Chris Woakes	25	8	61	3	2.44	0	0
Joe Root	7.1	1	20	2	2.79	0	0
Harry Brook	3	1	7	0	2.33	0	0

ENGLAND 2ND INNINGS

BATTING		R	B	M	4S	6S	SR
Zak Crawley	c Smith b Cummins	73	76	124	9	0	96.05
Ben Duckett	c †Carey b Starc	42	55	82	7	0	76.36
Ben Stokes (c)	c Cummins b Murphy	42	67	101	3	1	62.68
Joe Root	b Murphy	91	106	174	11	1	85.84
Harry Brook	c †Carey b Hazlewood	7	6	7	0	1	116.66
Jonny Bairstow †	c †Carey b Starc	78	103	136	11	0	75.72
Moeen Ali	c Hazlewood b Starc	29	38	57	4	0	76.31
Chris Woakes	c Khawaja b Starc	1	5	8	0	0	20.00
Mark Wood	c Marsh b Murphy	9	11	16	1	0	81.81
Stuart Broad	not out	8	8	28	0	1	100.00
James Anderson	lbw b Murphy	8	19	22	2	0	42.10
Extras	(lb 4, nb 3)	7					
TOTAL	81.5 Ov (RR: 4.82)	395					

Fall of wickets: 1-79 (Ben Duckett, 16.6 ov), 2-140 (Zak Crawley, 26.3 ov), 3-213 (Ben Stokes, 39.3 ov), 4-222 (Harry Brook, 40.5 ov), 5-332 (Joe Root, 65.3 ov), 6-360 (Jonny Bairstow, 72.4 ov), 7-364 (Chris Woakes, 74.1 ov), 8-375 (Moeen Ali, 76.6 ov), 9-379 (Mark Wood, 77.2 ov), 10-395 (James Anderson, 81.5 ov)

BOWLING	O	M	R	W	ECON	WD	NB
Mitchell Starc	20	2	100	4	5.00	0	0
Josh Hazlewood	15	0	67	1	4.46	0	1
Pat Cummins	16	0	79	1	4.93	0	1
Mitchell Marsh	8	0	35	0	4.37	0	1
Todd Murphy	22.5	0	110	4	4.81	0	0

AUSTRALIA 2ND INNINGS (T: 384 RUNS)

BATTING		R	B	M	4S	6S	SR
David Warner	c †Bairstow b Woakes	60	106	171	9	0	56.60
Usman Khawaja	lbw b Woakes	72	145	184	8	0	49.65
Marnus Labuschagne	c Crawley b Wood	13	33	38	2	0	39.39
Steven Smith	c Crawley b Woakes	54	94	142	9	0	57.44
Travis Head	c Root b Ali	43	70	107	6	0	61.42
Mitchell Marsh	c †Bairstow b Ali	6	9	9	1	0	66.66
Alex Carey †	c †Bairstow b Broad	28	50	83	1	1	56.00
Mitchell Starc	c Crawley b Woakes	0	2	3	0	0	0.00
Pat Cummins (c)	c Stokes b Ali	9	14	21	1	0	64.28
Todd Murphy	c †Bairstow b Broad	18	39	38	3	0	46.15
Josh Hazlewood	not out	4	8	13	1	0	50.00
Extras	(b 10, lb 10, nb 2, w 5)	27					
TOTAL	94.4 Ov (RR: 3.52)	334					

Fall of wickets: 1-140 (David Warner, 41.2 ov), 2-141 (Usman Khawaja, 43.2 ov), 3-169 (Marnus Labuschagne, 48.6 ov), 4-264 (Travis Head, 73.3 ov), 5-274(Steven Smith, 74.6 ov), 6-274 (Mitchell Marsh, 75.5 ov), 7-275 (Mitchell Starc, 76.3 ov), 8-294 (Pat Cummins, 81.2 ov), 9-329 (Todd Murphy, 90.6 ov), 10-334(Alex Carey, 94.4 ov)

BOWLING	O	M	R	W	ECON	WD	NB
Stuart Broad	20.4	4	62	2	3.00	0	0
James Anderson	14	4	53	0	3.78	0	1
Chris Woakes	19	4	50	4	2.63	0	1
Moeen Ali	23	2	76	3	3.30	0	0
Joe Root	9	0	39	0	4.33	0	0
Mark Wood	9	0	34	1	3.77	1	0

Summary

Ashes 2 Ashes

Just as well Ben Stokes' taboo on draws does not extend to series: we would have missed out at The Oval on a cracking Test match. But Stokes grasped the importance of a meaningful final word, and England played like a team that wanted to have it.

The last time the Ashes were squared, the scenario was similar. In 1972, England held the urn. They got mysteriously lucky in the Fourth Test on a pitch with a bizarre fungal affliction — the one fungal disease, fuserium, that every cricket fan knows. Derek Underwood lived up to his nickname of 'Deadly'.

As Australia arrived at The Oval to play a team with an unbeatable 2–1 series lead, they felt, as Dennis Lillee wrote, 'cheated'. Captain Ian Chappell and manager Ray Steele primed them to fight back. 'I think we are the better team, and if we go home two-all we will have been seen as the better team,' he counselled. Steele was even more succinct: 'Win here and we will be known as winners.'

Which is, indeed, the way that Test is remembered: as

heralding a great Australian era. And that may also prove true for Stokes' team, who have now won thirteen and lost four of their Tests under his leadership, in a vein whose appeal it is hard to dispute. Tripped up on the way out in these Ashes at Edgbaston and Lord's, they trampled Australia in the run home at Headingley, Old Trafford, and The Oval.

England's run rate, 4.74, was the highest in a series of more than four Tests *in history*. Let that sink in a moment. Their batters let go as a proportion half as many balls as their Australian counterparts, grudged a maiden only once every nineteen overs versus one in five. The contrast was sharpest between respective opening batters: whereas Usman Khawaja's 496 runs took him 1,263 balls, Zak Crawley's 480 took him 541.

Remember, too, that this was in the face of mainly defensive fields from Cummins—fields set to prevent boundaries, to discourage hitters. In fact, England took full advantage of the expanses that Cummins left untenanted in the hope of securing perimeters. Perhaps there was a feeling in the Australian camp that at some stage England were bound to blow up, that they couldn't keep playing the way they were, that opportunities would inevitably present themselves. If so, it turned into rope-a-dope for one. The stage never came. Australia had better and poorer days, but after Lord's, no outright winning ones.

Some argued as the series went on that England were taking so little time over their runs so as to be wasting opportunities to put overs in the Australians' legs. The contrary argument may hold more water. For Australia's bowlers, there was a feeling of constant pressure, that ordinary balls were bound for punishment, that not even good deliveries were safe, and that analyses would be unflattering—all of which takes a mental as well as a physical toll.

For Australia's fielders, there was a sense of always being

in the game wherever they were, of constantly being called on to anticipate, chase, dive, back up—T20 fielding, as it were, stretched over whole days. For Australia's captain, there was an uneasy sensation of not being in control of events, to which Pat Cummins is decidedly unused, especially once Nathan Lyon fell by the wayside.

So while it might be shorter, sharper, and less obviously attritional, Bazball remains gruelling to be on the end of. When five Test matches are packed in as tightly as these, furthermore, relief is scant. I'll say it once more for emphasis: this was a schedule that disgraced all those involved in designing it. Good luck with The Hundred. And get stuffed.

In winning the World Test Championship at the top of summer, the Australians set themselves a high standard to maintain. In fact, only Khawaja and the Mitchells, Starc and Marsh, were able to measure up—and Marsh had not even been expected to play a part in the series. Huge and hearty, he has always looked a slightly odd fit in Test cricket, as improbably dainty with the bat as a man eating pizza with a knife and fork. But his hundred at Headingley was the outstanding Australian innings of the series, and in the best three on either side. Travis Head gets a pass mark; Todd Murphy, a tick. But Cameron Green and Scott Boland failed to surmount the first obstacles they have encountered at Test level, and David Warner left England with the same questions that surrounded him on arrival.

England? That palpable back-end surge owed everything to the fresh legs of Chris Woakes and Mark Wood, who took 33 wickets between them in the three Tests at 19. To that point, Stuart Broad had really been running a one-man show, with Ollie Robinson and James Anderson off the boil: it was very Bazball that England's two least effective bowlers were their most economical. Woakes' craft, Wood's speed, and their tail-end runs lifted England a crucial cog.

Moeen, just, covered the absence of Jack Leach, and his unlikely contribution at number three was useful. But Stokes was missed with the ball, not least by Ben Foakes, against whose selection this militated. Bairstow finished the series on a positive note, but 82 byes reflects his keeping as much as his 24 dismissals, and in hindsight a five-Test series was a huge ask in view of his long prior break from the game. Had he caught Khawaja in the first over of the second innings at Edgbaston, and had he not wandered aimlessly from his crease at Lord's, how different this series might have been.

If Root at times started at a seeming hurry, he remains the standard bearer of English batsmanship, an enchantment to watch, finally achieving the Ashes results he would expect of himself. Crawley, however, was a revelation, very much a tone-setter and scene-shifter, with Duckett an admirable partner. It was puzzling that Australia did not bowl short to Crawley more often, although his height would make this challenging. His overall record remains disarmingly modest, but his peaks are potentially match-winning, and his leadership possibilities loom larger now than Ollie Pope's. Brook may not quite have made the runs expected, but he made them in the fashion foretold.

In some ways, every player in England's team leads you back to contemplating Stokes, and way he has imbued them with his peculiar gusto. He is a remarkable sight: that weightlifter's torso, those matelot's arms, and that face like the portrait of one of Elizabeth I's courtiers, at least if bucket hats had then been in favour. Perhaps that is a key to his appeal, which seems to connect with every fan, despite English cricket's renownedly stratified nature. England has always required a minimum of polish from its captains: you can't see Andrew Strauss or Alastair Cook in a bucket hat, can you? Nor did leadership agree with either of Stokes' great all-round predecessors, Sir Ian Botham or Andrew Flintoff. But even when he is not bowling, England's skipper compels reverence without demanding it, which is how the best leaders hold us in thrall.

PLAYERS' AVERAGES

AUSTRALIA BATTING AVERAGES

PLAYER	MAT	INNS	NO	RUNS	HS	AVE	SR	100	50
MR Marsh	3	6	1	250	118	50.00	66.84	1	1
UT Khawaja	5	10	0	496	141	49.60	39.27	1	3
SPD Smith	5	10	0	373	110	37.29	56.09	1	2
TM Head	5	10	0	362	77	36.20	71.11	-	3
M Labuschagne	5	10	0	328	111	32.79	46.99	1	1
DA Warner	5	10	0	285	66	28.50	56.21	-	2
PJ Cummins	5	9	2	162	44*	23.14	52.09	-	-
AT Carey	5	9	0	200	66	22.22	47.96	-	1
C Green	3	6	1	103	38	20.60	41.53	-	-
T Murphy	2	4	0	76	34	19.00	76.00	-	-
MA Starc	4	7	2	82	36*	16.39	42.70	-	-
SM Boland	2	4	2	20	20	10.00	40.00	-	-
NM Lyon	2	4	1	28	16*	9.33	46.66	-	-
JR Hazlewood	4	6	3	20	6*	6.66	43.47	-	-

AUSTRALIA BOWLING AVERAGES

PLAYER	MAT	OVERS	MDNS	RUNS	WKTS	BBI	AVE	ECON	SR	5	10
T Murphy	2	38.2	-	181	7	4/110	25.85	4.72	32.8	-	-
MA Starc	4	128.1	8	623	23	5/78	27.08	4.86	33.4	1	-
NM Lyon	2	66.0	4	264	9	4/80	29.33	4.00	44.0	-	-
JR Hazlewood	4	111.0	5	507	16	5/126	31.68	4.56	41.6	1	-
PJ Cummins	5	158.4	8	679	18	6/91	37.72	4.27	52.8	1	-
TM Head	5	18.0	1	92	2	2/17	46.00	5.11	54.0	-	-
C Green	3	45.4	4	235	5	2/64	47.00	5.14	54.8	-	-
MR Marsh	3	34.0	1	167	3	1/9	55.66	4.91	68.0	-	-
SM Boland	2	47.0	3	231	2	1/61	115.50	4.91	141.0	-	-
SPD Smith	5	1.0	-	1	0	-	-	1.00	-	-	-
M Labuschagne	5	1.0	-	3	0	-	-	3.00	-	-	-
AT Carey	5	0.0	-	-	0	-	-	-	-	-	-
UT Khawaja	5	0.0	-	-	0	-	-	-	-	-	-
DA Warner	5	0.0	-	-	0	-	-	-	-	-	-

ENGLAND BATTING AVERAGES

PLAYER	MAT	INNS	NO	RUNS	HS	AVE	SR	100	50
Z Crawley	5	9	0	480	189	53.33	88.72	1	2
JE Root	5	9	1	412	118*	51.50	74.77	1	2
BA Stokes	5	9	0	405	155	45.00	64.69	1	2
HC Brook	5	9	0	363	85	40.33	78.74	-	4
JM Bairstow	5	9	1	322	99*	40.25	77.03	-	3
BM Duckett	5	9	0	321	98	35.66	75.88	-	2
MM Ali	4	7	0	180	54	25.71	65.21	-	1
OJ Pope	2	4	0	90	42	22.50	67.66	-	-
MA Wood	3	5	1	83	28	20.75	129.68	-	-
CR Woakes	3	5	1	79	36	19.75	79.79	-	-
OE Robinson	3	5	2	59	27	19.66	60.82	-	-
SCJ Broad	5	8	2	78	16	13.00	55.31	-	-
JC Tongue	1	2	0	20	19	10.00	66.66	-	-
JM Anderson	4	6	3	28	12	9.33	35.89	-	-

ENGLAND BOWLING AVERAGES

PLAYER	MAT	OVERS	MDNS	RUNS	WKTS	BBI	AVE	ECON	SR	5	10
CR Woakes	3	113.2	22	345	19	5/62	**18.14**	3.04	35.7	1	-
MA Wood	3	87.4	15	283	14	5/34	**20.21**	3.22	37.5	1	-
OE Robinson	3	102.4	28	284	10	3/55	**28.40**	2.76	61.6	-	-
SCJ Broad	5	184.2	33	625	22	4/65	**28.40**	3.39	50.2	-	-
JE Root	5	53.1	8	172	6	2/19	**28.66**	3.23	53.1	-	-
BA Stokes	5	29.0	4	89	3	1/9	**29.66**	3.06	58.0	-	-
JC Tongue	1	42.0	7	151	5	3/98	**30.20**	3.59	50.4	-	-
MM Ali	4	126.0	15	463	9	3/76	**51.44**	3.67	84.0	-	-
JM Anderson	4	154.0	37	427	5	1/51	**85.40**	2.77	184.8	-	-
HC Brook	5	6.0	2	12	0	-	-	2.00	-	-	-
JM Bairstow	5	0.0	-	-	0	-	-	-	-	-	-
Z Crawley	5	0.0	-	-	0	-	-	-	-	-	-
BM Duckett	5	0.0	-	-	0	-	-	-	-	-	-
OJ Pope	2	0.0	-	-	0	-	-	-	-	-	-

Acknowledgements

Tour books are passé. Everyone knows that. I had no thought of putting this book together until after the First Test. I considered it more seriously after the Second, and then more seriously again after the Third. By then, emails were arriving: would there be a book? At which point, Henry Rosenbloom, publisher of *A Fair Field and No Favour*, my 2005 Ashes travelogue, popped in with the same question. So, first of all, thanks everyone for *Ashes 2023: a cricket classic*. I couldn't — wouldn't — have done it without you.

Notwithstanding my strictures, the Aussie press pack and the English media corps managed to make this a fun tour. There remains a durable sense of being there because we want to be, and then everyone agrees afterwards that it's been the best tour ever — the 2023 Ashes was no exception. Whatever the annoyances of being on the road, it's sure as hell better than languishing in an office. Someone had to do that languishing for us, of course, and I'm glad it was Tom Clarke and James Restall at *The Times*, and Steve Samuelsen and Chris Stedman at *The Australian*.

Along the way, there was much kindness from old friends. Mike Atherton hosted me with his usual kindness and solicitude during the two longer breaks. Charlie Connelly, Tom Holland,

and the Authors XI made me welcome on the field. There was a chance to catch up with Murali Krishna, Prudence Fay, Joe Aston, Dominic Lawson, Mick Herron, Ed Caesar, Bernard Fanning, Stephanie Bunbury, and multiple members of the Yarras, to visit the Chalke Valley History Festival and Marylebone's excellent symposium on cricket tours and empire organised by Neil Robinson. But, of course, to nobody do I owe more thanks than Peter Lalor, my colleague and friend for twelve great years. With whom else could you watch a day of cricket, pay homage to the favourite watering holes of Mark E. Smith because of a shared affinity for The Fall, and/or detour to Crossness Engines in Abbey Wood out of a mutual interest in sewers? Podcasts in pubs and taxis, by roadsides and on trains? Why not? We hope you enjoyed *Cricket Et Cetera*, the sound of two middle-aged white men trying to find the on-switch, as much as we enjoyed making it.